I've Got a Story to Tell

Studies in the
Postmodern Theory of Education

Joe L. Kincheloe and Shirley R. Steinberg
General Editors

Vol. 65

PETER LANG
New York • Washington, D.C./Baltimore • Boston
Bern • Frankfurt am Main • Berlin • Vienna • Paris

I've Got a Story to Tell

Identity and Place in the Academy

Edited by
Sandra Jackson
and José Solís Jordán

PETER LANG
New York • Washington, D.C./Baltimore • Boston
Bern • Frankfurt am Main • Berlin • Vienna • Paris

Library of Congress Cataloging-in-Publication Data

I've got a story to tell: identity and place
in the academy / edited by Sandra Jackson and José Solís Jordán.
p. cm. — (Counterpoints; v. 65)
Includes bibliographical references.
1. Minorities—Education (Higher)—United States—Case studies.
2. Minority college teachers—United States—Case studies.
3. Multicultural education—United States—Case studies. I. Jackson, Sandra.
II. Solís Jordán, José. III. Series: Counterpoints (New York, N.Y.); vol. 65.
LC3731.I94   371.829—dc21   97-25670
ISBN 0-8204-3862-6
ISSN 1058-1634

Die Deutsche Bibliothek-CIP-Einheitsaufnahme

I've got a story to tell: identity and place in the academy / ed. by Sandra Jackson and José
Solís Jordán.–New York; Washington, D.C./Baltimore; Boston; Bern;
Frankfurt am Main; Berlin; Vienna; Paris: Lang.
(Counterpoints; Vol. 65)
ISBN 0-8204-3862-6

Cover design by Nona Reuter.

The paper in this book meets the guidelines for permanence and durability
of the Committee on Production Guidelines for Book Longevity
of the Council of Library Resources.

© 1999 Peter Lang Publishing, Inc., New York

Printed in the United States of America.

Acknowledgments

When we began to talk about and reflect upon our experiences in the academy, we knew that we were on to something and began to consider the potential of inquiry into the experiences of others like ourselves—Others in the academy. We decided to engage colleagues in dialogue about the meanings of being in higher education and negotiating space and places to be. This book is the result of exchanges and dialogues about the experiences of faculty of color in higher education and the multiplicity of ways in which individuals attend to the subjectivities of their experiences rooted in issues related to identity and the professorate, with particular attention to relationships with students and colleagues within institutional contexts.

Without the contributions of those whose voices speak through this text, this book would have not been possible. We therefore extend our deepest appreciation to the authors who have been willing to speak of the personal in public, sharing their experiences in ways we hope will provide insight into what it means for us: the Natives in the academy. We offer this work as an engagement in the on-going conversation about the academy and difference. We dedicate this work to those who will come after us, and continue the work of those who have come before us in struggle to assure that our presence and the voices of people like us, our ideas, and contributions to the construction of knowledge and education of others are included in that which is considered worthy of knowing.

We have many individuals to thank in supporting our work to bring this project to fruition. On the production side, we express our gratitude to Mervin Mendez and Maria Vasquez who worked the text, read it and put into shape. We also acknowledge the University Research Council at DePaul University, Chicago, for granting us funding so that

we could finalize the preparation of the manuscript. We especially thank our editor, Christopher Myers at Peter Lang who amicably shepheded us through the process; Joe Kincheloe and Shirley R. Steinberg, the series editors, who believed in the idea of the book; to Scott Gillam who cleaned up the text and suggested some very helpful revisions and yet honored each voice; and the production manager, Nona Reuter, who finalized preparation of the manuscript for publication; to those who reviewed the book, Cameron McCarthy, Felix Padilla and Christine E. Sleeter, in particular, as well as others who read the manuscript in whole or in part and provided helpful comments.

Work like this consumes time and encroaches upon family life. To each of our spouses, Fassil Demissie and Martha Gonzalez, we are indebted for their support and encouragement at every stage of this project.

Table of Contents

Introduction

Being in Higher Education: Negotiating Identity and Place

Sandra Jackson and José Solís Jordán

Our collection of narratives strives to further the discourse regarding the multiple interrelationships of identity, self, others, pedagogy, and institutions of higher learning. The accounts that follow describe what it means to be a professor within the contested terrain of higher education, to break silences, and to speak of the unspeakable: the subjectivities of women and men of color as educators contending with issues of race, gender, and class in their personal and pedagogical practices. Although a number of other texts in the recent literature have included similar narratives or accounts, few have (re)presented the treatment of identity and teaching with a focus upon professors of color.

Through the voices of such women and men in higher education, we have invoked truth telling and critical interrogation of their lived experiences as teachers through narrative accounts of their teaching. Through storytelling—multicultural, gendered, and classed—the contributors to this text bring the experience of teachers of color to the center of discourse regarding identity, teaching, the politics of difference, and the creation of spaces and places through which the exercise of agency is made manifest within institutions of higher learning.

This book is about education experienced by professors of color in the academy and the persistence of difference negotiated within multilayered contexts involving administration, peers, students, curriculum, and pedagogy. Each of the individuals who have contributed to this collection of narratives has, in gaining a doctoral degree, on the surface acquired that which should have garnered them currency within higher education, as well as within larger social contexts, given the promise of education as the "great equalizer." Yet, what the stories reveal is that masked beneath the facade of opportunity, blemishes remain and persist which make one's experiences richly nuanced and inevitably problematic regarding issues of identity, one's presence, practices, and the politics of difference where who one is, what and how one teaches is inextricably tied to the dynamic between self and others and institutional articulations of power and knowledge.

The experiences of those few, from diverse communities of color who have ostensibly been successful academically, stand in sharp contrast to experiences of people of color in general throughout the United States, where debates and struggles about equality of opportunity, quality of educational experiences, high dropout rates, and inadequate facilities and equipment persist. In public education for children and youth as well as in higher education, social, cultural, linguistic, racial, class, and gender issues remain salient concerns of people of color. Upon entry to the academy as a faculty member, the scholar of color quickly learns that these very issues permeate the environment and are refracted through their own experiences there. The stories herein speak of this environment, with professors of color as players, articulating pain as well as resistance in overcoming and transformation in places where the desert's hot dry air drains one of energy, burning the brain, stupefying the senses, only to be replaced by the mirage of sustenance.

Like an oasis, *I've Got a Story to Tell* presents what the editors consider to be a refreshing well of voices amidst the often desertlike environment of higher education. The contributors to this book, like so many other academics of color, while "successful," are nonetheless faced with the same White supremacy, sexism, racism, and homophobia confronting people of color beyond the campus walls. Yet for the contributors working within these very walls, there reside possibilities. For the contributors, this text is a place, indeed a space, wherein the contributors can momentarily unload the baggage they carry and speak incisively of the challenges associated with their success in gaining entry into the academy.

This book of stories by professors of color discloses issues of the heart and the soul regarding how faculty of color negotiate issues of race, gender, sexuality, and authority in their professional lives. Grounded in critical reflection of lived experiences, these stories legitimate the perspectives told in the language and tenor of the signifiers and the particular situatedness of their positions. Invoking subjectivity and positionality subverts traditional discursive practices wherein objectivity and distance are privileged—creating a dynamic which abstracts experiences and blinds one by the fury of the stinging winds of negation. What the narratives in this collection seek to do is not to affirm that experience is the only way of knowing, but rather to ascribe meanings forged from the worlds and in the words of the storytellers on their own terms.

Through candor and clarity, a genuine language and linguistic dynamic is forged by an approach that reenforces the humanization of the storyteller otherwise muted and distorted by attempts to marginalize and dismiss. In this regard, the stories of contending with White supremacy and homophobia in *I've Got a Story to Tell* challenge us to disarm ourselves of the often comfortable languages that limit the possibilities for transforming our world and our words. Or again, the stories might compel us to retreat, reaching into a closet of language, searching frantically in hopes that the power of the story as lived and known to the teller can be diluted by an official language of meanings, and of meanings of meanings, until the experience is abstracted, eviscerated of organic meaning(s), until there is no humanity to the experience, nothing that should necessarily move one to struggle to understand the experiences of others who are different.

Because of the barriers confronting scholars and professors of color in higher education, it is not uncommon for us to articulate that in a real sense we have learned how not to talk (about issues of race, sexuality, and gender) because of the fiercely political, social, and cultural environment of the academy, which impinges upon one's experiences in relationship to one's peers, students, as well as administrators regarding not only the curriculum but also pedagogy, scholarship, promotion, tenure—indeed one's very existence there. The very idea of engaging in dialogue is often perceived as a way to reconcile differences. But reconciliation is often construed to be and used as a means to resolve differences in a manner which reestablishes the myth of facile cooperation by appealing to notions such as compromise, middleground, and neutrality—all predicated upon sustaining the status- quo regarding relations of power and knowledge. This makes the possibility of "honest dialogue" problematic; hence, the commensurability of differences vis-à-vis dialogical exercises remains as perplexing as ever. Yet assuming that one arrives at a point where dialogue can take place, assuming that such is possible, the question of respect and trust must be addressed.

Too often professors of color are accused of being overly sensitive, without humor, taking things too seriously, and looking for trouble where none exists when they address issues regarding race, for example, because they cannot possibly be objective—being too close to the controversy and therefore perceived as acting out of a narrow and limited self-interest. In the classroom this dynamic is played out in differential responses by students to faculty of color and White faculty. For example, in a critical examination of let us say inequality, when a White professor presents an argument or a given way to look at an issue, he (more often than she) is presumed to be objective, having grounded whatever analysis in fact. However, a faculty member of color, attempting to engage in critical interrogation of issues related to race (among other things) is invariably presumed by students to be biased, overly sensitive, presenting arguments with questionable merit. The same dynamic is played out regarding White colleagues and administrators regarding faculty of color. While not necessarily explicitly articulated when conflicts emerge, in these defining moments, reified objectivity is invoked and individuals of color are implicitly challenged to see things from the perspectives of others—while others may eschew theirs—all in the name of "can't we just get along?" The good of the group, in which the person of color is inevitably among those underrepresented, is privileged, and the language of putting feelings aside to benefit all is used as a tool to negate claims of the so-called special interest groups, while at the same time persons of color are expected to desist in being the noisy wheel and to work to resolve matters in ways which often circumvent confronting and engaging in conflict necessary to forge authentic understandings and genuine consensus where possible.

Such imperatives in institutions of higher education make the development of a climate of trust nigh impossible. For oppression gives birth to strategies of resistance and acts of liberation which collide with the need to control and maintain the order of things by establishing parameters of definitions and protocols for action which do not accommodate the needs of diverse parties. It should be no surprise then that faculty of color within these contexts ask themselves, "But how can I trust the master?" How can the master trust me? Knowing that, as Audre Lorde has said, one cannot use the master's tools to dismantle the master's house, what results is engagement in communicative acts and not necessarily dialogues across experiences of difference. This state of affairs creates formidable challenges for any professor of color, particularly young, nontenured professors. In higher education, these barriers are amplified by the manner in which the legitimacy and authority of the professors of color is questioned or challenged by their peers, who question their research and scholarship and make decisions about tenure and promotion; by students, who question their knowledge and pedagogical practices; and by administrators, who make judgments about recruitment, hiring, and promotion and tenure,and about how differences are resolved when conflicts manifest themselves around issues of race, gender, class, language, and culture. It should be no surprise, then, that articulations of lived experiences in the academy reverberate the hurt and anger over the persistence of White supremacy and systems of control against which individuals must struggle daily.

As with other bureaucratic organizations, within the academy power is articulated vertically. Changes come from above. And even when a change is ushered in and presented as benefiting the populations of color on a campus, it is presented as if it is simply the prerogative of decision makers up above, instead of the result of advocacy, challenge, and struggle engaged in by persons of color and their allies among faculty, students, as well as the larger communities which surround campuses. Student activism regarding hate speech, rape, violence on campus as well as acts of discrimination and bigotry, along with faculty challenges to discrimination in promotion and hiring decisions, often result in token responses from university officials: a tenure decision here and there overturned; recruitment of a few more students of color; some increase in financial aid for a few more students of color; inclusion of a gay or lesbian hire in the applicant pool for an open position; and celebrations and related social activities around Black History Month, or Latino or Asian Week. Treated in this manner, conflict resolution is done in such a way that fundamental practices and belief systems within the academy remain virtually unchanged.

Official discourse within the academy requires the maintenance of a relationship between the perceived need to maintain a tradition of epistemological hierarchies while simultaneously making symbolic gestures affirming the legitimacy of difference or diversity. The notion that a center be maintained to which the Others are peripheral—marginalized and trivialized—reveals not only the hegemonic problems inherent in the traditional epistemological stance, but also discloses a real fear that is associated with the decentering of its own stance. Arguments at this nexus often quickly become consumed within the logic of binary opposition—either-or—and a war of words and worlds ensues. When conflict emerges, often the response is choreographed like a dance to mute it and make it palatable, render it controllable and acceptable. Here narratives can serve to be disruptive of official discourse through the insurgence of particular voices which speak the unspeakable. Through such narratives we are challenged to reconsider the existent relations of power and engagement and the possibilities of understanding the constructed nature of knowledge. Through their multivocality, the narratives included in this collection question received knowledge, linear constructions of knowing, and fixed meanings. The possibilities of making horizontal the vertical tradition of epistemological hierarchy has potentially democratizing effects in leveling the discursive field.

Speaking against the grain, subverting marginalization and trivialization, the narratives in *I've Got a Story to Tell* discuss and comment upon the situated dynamics of being of color and teaching in what remains predominantly white institutions of higher learning. The tenor of the multiple voices is insurgent and transgressive, not in the language of the complaint but in the argument inscribed in the struggle for pedagogies that transcend the boundaries of comfort zones. What one hears in these narratives is not about feeling good, not about feeling bad; rather they are about feeling deeply and responding to the politics of constraint, suppression, repression, coercion, and conformity. Collectively the contributors to this book speak frankly and unabashedly about their experiences in the academy. They call for a broad and inclusive examination of the persistent problems in academe and at the same time affirm the legitimacy of professors and scholars of color: who we are, what we teach and how we teach.

Professors of color are often conspicuous in their limited if not singular presence on faculties of higher education. Their work as educators is tempered by the baggage they bring as well as their relationships with their peers, students and administration. While their experiences in some ways are similar to those of others who teach and are affected by issues of authority and legitimacy, issues of difference and conflict are exacerbated when the professor is one of color, gendered, and classed, and whose language and sexual orientation make him or her decidedly the other. One's location is mediated by the nexus of multiple aspects of identity refracted in a particular set of circumstances regarding teaching and learning.

I've Got a Story to Tell brings forth and shares with the reader the words and experiences of the worlds of the contributors. These stories are not meant to be taken to represent or speak of any essentialisms, or make universal claims either epistemologically or ontologically about faculty and scholars of color. Rather, they attest to the richly textured and diverse experiences of individuals from diverse backgrounds—ethnically and culturally—told to "your face" with the hope of eye-to-eye engagement. These stories are shared with the intent to invite thoughtful reflection and deliberation about what it means to be, to struggle, to transform self and others in the practice of freedom in teaching and learning in higher education.

Chapter 1

Why Are You So Afraid, Güero?

José Solís Jordán

The stillness of the pool water mirrored the tranquility of the environment that surrounded us. I was one of maybe three people outside
absorbing the Mayan sun's heat while captivated by the whispers of
the wind as it passed among the branches of the abundant trees high
above. An occasional leaf would drift ever so slowly as if deliberating
each turn and twist of its vertical trajectory down into the water where
it would rest, creating the sublest of ripples in the pool. I was mesmer-
ized by the beauty, calm, and power of that day. I thought to myself,
"What discipline, what strength and resolve, what magnificence of
organization and culture." Temples of stone ascended across the land-
scape. Affirming the presence of voices, of memory, and of civilization, these rock ruins appeared not as if they had been buried but
instead as if they were being born from the womb of the earth, push-
ing forward and upward to once again reveal the grandeur of the Mayan
peoples. The pyramids, so tall and so accurate, dwarfed anything in
sight. Their rock construction coupled with the architectural design
and aesthetic composition proudly proclaimed that there was no doubt
that these were a great people with a magnificent culture and civilization. How did they do this? What happened? In some ways I wanted
to better understand how the power of memory had been attacked
and stripped from the Mexicano people. What a pedagogical process
it must have been to develop such a culture. What a project it must
have been to attempt its annihilation.

The surface of the pool water became my mantra, a kind of noth-
ingness in which my thoughts and feelings could maintain an
indisturbable focus, a place from which my senses could travel freely
as I absorbed the environment, each thought, smell, and sensation
driven by my awe at the wonder of the Maya. Suddenly, as if awakened

by a boulder falling out of the sky into the pool water, I heard a voice assert angrily, "Dr. Solís, I can't believe what just happened." Torn from my moment of reflection, I listened as the student recounted what she had just experienced.

The foreign study group from the university at which I taught had just completed one of numerous excursions to different anthropological and archeological sites in the Yucatán, in the southeastern part of México. Uxmal (one of the many principal archeological and anthropological sites of the Maya) was the subject of my amazement. After a tour of the site, we were to have dinner at a restaurant just outside the area. A number of students from our university were fixed on watching television. It was Super Bowl Sunday. The student that approached me recounted the experience in the restaurant. The management at the restaurant was kind enough to provide the students with a television in order to watch the game. As with most sporting events, the game opened with a rendition of the United States national anthem. What shocked the student, and myself after hearing about it, was how some members of the group used the context of the game and the national anthem to reinforce their sense of power and superiority. Those participating sang along with the national anthem very loudly and forcefully.

The student who had brought the incident to my attention shared that she was appalled and hurt since the workers and management in the restaurant were indigenous and understood what was happening. To me it was not a moment of national reflection and affirmation. The act was loaded with the baggage of racist values (and miseducation) these students had internalized. The restaurant was a public site. There were people in the restaurant that, having nothing to do with the group, witnessed this display of disrespect. They remained silent yet observant. I wondered, after I went into the restaurant, what the workers in there were thinking. It reminded me of the visions that one conjures up of fascists proclaiming their power over others and through such an act, appropriating the moment in order to reaffirm their dominance over the "other," over Mexicanos and anyone else who would dare to question their power.

But this moment had its precedents; and my story is about the experiences with the foreign study program in the Yucatán that forced these students to reveal their racism and the racism I encountered when attempting to engage in a transformative anti-racist pedagogy.

The university at which I taught had invited me to direct the foreign study program in Mérida, in the state of Yucatán, in México, during a winter quarter. I designed and developed a class and planned different trips to a variety of places in southeastern México. The course title was Identity and Development: The Yucatán. The general idea behind the course was to critically examine how and why we construct our definitions and conceptualizations of what development is, and the import of our identity formation as it informs our sense of development. The subheading of the course gave the study its context. The class would address the experiences of contemporary México and the Yucatán throughout the quarter. A number of students in our group knew me from my work at the School of Education. A few, who had even taken classes with me before and discovered that I was to be the field director for the program during the following quarter, expressed their interest in participating in the program. The group was quite diverse. We had students from commerce, education, political science, women's studies, Latin American studies, and international marketing, to mention a few. We also had a diverse group racially. African-Americans, Whites, a Filipino, and Mexicanos made up the group. The vast majority was Mexicano.

The history of the Foreign Study Program had unfortunately given the students the impression that a quarter abroad in the Yucatán was equivalent to ten weeks of vacation with easy courses for credit to satisfy the education side of things. This was, I believe, in part due to the "party" factor emphasized by so many former participants and the lack of seriousness and discipline in the program's pedagogical framework. In addition to the logistical orientation, and the cultural awareness games we played prior to our departure, I requested that the entire group meet to discuss feelings and thoughts on the topics to be studied prior to the trip. I was never given the time I needed to engage with the students in an appropriate manner other than in a most superficial and passing way. Virtually all of the pre-departure meetings concentrated on logistical matters. I did tell the students that they would not be the same after a quarter in México.

In Mérida, the students took different classes. They were placed in an appropriate level Spanish class. The students were also enrolled in a Mayan anthropology course and some took Mexican history. All of the students were required to take my course. And so our quarter began.

I do not believe any of them were prepared for the experiences they encountered in my class. We had readings on theories of development and questions of identity. But the readings were not what the class was about. The readings merely offered us some discursive tools

for engaging in the broader and more local concerns with development and identity. The class focused on discussions about ourselves
and the notion of "otherness" in México. Within the first week, a
group of White students in the class became quite uncomfortable with
the course. No one ever attacked them; yet their sense of power had
been challenged. I was quite candid in reaffirming that nothing would
be assumed or taken for granted in our class. What made the journey
into self-reflection more difficult was the realization that, in México,
they lacked the social force of the White dominant (U.S.) society at
their backs to sustain their myths of power and superiority over others. There was a part of me that believed that such a geographical
change would help them with their disease. But they continued to
resist.

I had prepared readings on the North American Free Trade Agreement (NAFTA) from which to look at some of México's most current
issues in the area of development. This small, but as I and others
would soon discover, vociferous group, felt very uneasy with the readings. At worst, they felt criticism of NAFTA was merely subjective
conjecture, lacking objectivity. At best, they were cynical about the
reality of the Mexicano people and their experiences, particularly its
indigenous struggles. Much of their concern was relayed to me by
other members of the group. I remember being told that this small
group was afraid that I would have an impact on the group and influence its members. I understood clearly that this was merely a way of
first attempting to absolve themselves from having to support an argument or critique and, second, surrendering to reactionary postur-
ing. I imagined they felt that there was no way the master race was
going to have to reason before its subordinates.

Their geographical change of space from Chicago to México, in
their eyes, did not make them the "other." As Fanon has articulated,
the "other" is not other to the White; and White is its own other,
never having to depend on Blackness to be White. Such a deep-seated
racism cannot be challenged by spatial transfer. In México, Mexicanos
to these students were still not existential beings, but the fabrication
of an objectified "it" assigned a "they" category.

Our discussions about the suffering that México was experiencing
were very intense and sophisticated. Yet once the dialogue reached a
critical pitch, these students retreated into the world of that's-just-the-
way-it-is(ness). My critique of U.S. policy in México never motivated
these students to research and raise questions with my positions. I

imagined that consistent with notions of the master's narrative, they did not have to challenge, for that would merely have legitimized the claims raised by such critique.

The ten weeks of fun-in-the-sun had melted down into heat in the street. This small group of students would call home (Chicago) and the university expressing their concern with the course and the program in the Yucatán. A pretext that would facilitate the manufacture of the perception that I was the problem was needed; and was soon manufactured. As I have mentioned, the course began very deliberately and to some shockingly, since I had made it clear to the students that they were going to work and engage with the people of México. This would not be a vacation.

Prior to our departure, the participants and myself were told that excursions and trips during the quarter would be designed and developed by the students, myself, and the person in Mérida with whom our university had been working for some ten years. The person in the Yucatán and I exchanged many faxes, letters, and conversations on the topic of trips. I wanted all trips to be related to the educational experience, reinforcing a critical understanding of the themes studied in the classes. As we would later find out, our university had preplanned all of the excursions and any misunderstanding was their "oversight." This point became a real problem for the majority of the group and me.

Once in the Yucatán, the students demanded that the promise to be included in determinations regarding their money, as it related to trips and excursions, be honored. The principal issue centered on their desire to visit San Cristóbal de Las Casas, in Chiapas. One year earlier Chiapas had experienced an uprising by the Ejército Zapatista de Liberación Nacional (EZLN). Our university articulated that such a trip would depend upon my sense of the situation in Chiapas and the political atmosphere. Obviously, this was not true since the trip became an issue for our university once we were in México, and not while in Chicago discussing it prior to our departure to México. Furthermore, the focus of the problem was no longer security but finances, especially since the students and myself had not been told that the money for their trips was already committed.

For nearly two weeks, the group engaged in intense conversations and meetings on the topic of the trip. I told them that I would investigate matters related to security and finances. Once all was cleared for the trip, our university did its best to keep the students from seeing something other than pyramids, flamingos, and beach resorts. The students generally were angered by the deceit of the university, saying that such an underhanded tactic was not going to stop them. I agreed that the university had created a serious problem, undermining the confidence and trust needed to make this program successful. The group then discussed the logistics of a trip to Chiapas and whether everyone wanted to go. Interestingly, it turns out that the same small group at the core of the incident at the restaurant in Uxmal decided not to enter what one of them referred to as a "red zone" (Chiapas).

I knew that a White professor would not have experienced the insidiousness of the racism exhibited by these students. As a Latino, I challenged them. As a critical Latino scholar and professor, I had become a threat. This sentiment, I soon discovered, would be shared by the administration of the foreign study program.

The experience in Chiapas was very moving. Our group met numerous persons working with church organizations dedicated to social justice for the indigenous. San Cristóbal de las Casas is one of Mexico's most beautiful towns, exhibiting rich evidence of Spanish colonial and indigenous cultures. Such wealth attracts visitors from around the world, as we discovered, having run into Australians, Germans, Canadians, and U.S. Americans. Without a doubt, the trip to Chiapas was an experience that transformed all those who participated. I remember vividly when entering into the state of Chiapas, that the students were silent and in awe of the beauty and diversity reflected in the noticeable difference from Mérida in the Yucatán.

I will never forget my own emotions, having read the narratives they composed after the trip. I too was silenced, hypnotized by the lessons embedded in their stories on the meaning of the trip to Chiapas. Life now had a broader meaning. Baptized by the knowing of experience, the tools and concepts with which we measure the definitions of existence and how we understood others were deconstructed, and recreated by a conceptual lens forged by each student's sense of the journey.

Upon our return to Mérida, those that had not made the trip demonstrated mixed feelings about their decision. While they acknowledged that they would have liked to participate, their reasons for not going remained puzzling. I was always convinced that the White students in the group felt intimidated by the Latino and African-American students. Not two months prior to the trip, the director of the program, on different occasions, mentioned that this group was "quite intelligent and aware." I could not have agreed more. Yet the intellectual vivaciousness and critical thinking capabilities of the Latinos and African-Americans in the group would be interpreted as problems. Not ready to unreflectively accept the master's narrative regarding the identity and development of México, those who participated on the Chiapas trip soon became the targets of cynical interrogation. And, according to the White students, it was my responsibility to intervene and create a state of equilibrium in what they identified as prejudices and biases against them.

For the White students in the group, unfortunately, this affront to the master's tools challenged them to realize that any position taken was subject to critique. Yet, again, I sense that the White students expected that their Whiteness and the myths of their historically verified superiority were not be questioned. Racism became the surrogate for any intelligible inquiry. I understood that these students were experiencing what apparently they had never before considered—the possibility that they are one center of many different centers. Recognition and acknowledgment of this possibility, however, was not available to them. Theirs was a fear—a kind of paranoia that accompanies the insecurities of those whose identity thrives on the domination of others. They feared not me, not others, but what others and what I might offer them in understanding themselves. They feared that any attempt to shake them loose from their lockjaw-like grip on the dominant version of the world was tantamount to chaos, internal and social. My unwillingness to play the part of the anesthetist was seen as support for the Latino and African-American students. Any legitimization of the voices of "others" became synonymous with expressions of irrationality and little more than the echoing of incantations drummed into the minds of Latinos because they were Mexicanos, or Panamanians, or African-Americans acting in solidarity with the oppressed Mexicano peoples.

The fears, insecurities, and sense of alienation and loneliness, heightened by the White students' perceived need to frame the study of identity in terms of "us" and "them," exacerbated the bigotry contaminating their persons. Being in another land where their comfort zones had been shattered by both the place and those with whom they studied, compelled them to seek refuge and reaffirmation.

I sought repeatedly to discuss their difficulties with them. But how does a Latino professor discuss racism, even in private, with racist students? As a Latino educator, seeking a dialogue on racism with

White people is often akin to the doctor searching for a way to tell the patient that they have cancer. We know there is a deadly illness present, because we have experienced the evidence. The diseased feels nothing, sees nothing, and so assumes all is "normal" until the bad news is disclosed. And even then, the reactions may vary, but acceptance is difficult and often indefinitely ignored. Moreover, there remains the need to understand the relations of power present in the Latino professor/White student equation. While a White professor engaging in the study of racism engages in the study of self with others like him/her, when the Latino professor engages White students in the study of racism, each engages in the study of each other. The White professor/White student study of racism is incapable of transcending the assumptions about self or likeness, because in such a study no one present has experienced the receiving side of racism. Attempts to empathize tend only to reflect an abstraction of the pain and real experiences of people victimized by racism. Such an abstraction becomes a kind of warm place where we can ideationalize the problem and so, too, its resolution. Furthermore, there is not present the threat or challenge that comes from having to legitimize the "others" discourse. Whereas in the Latino professor/White student study of racism, the discourse of the "other" is forced into legitimacy by the power vested in the role of professor. This can make the study of racism most uncomfortable for the White student. Racism here is examined from the perspective of each toward the other.

The White student seeks assurance that the Latino professor will be objective and fair in his deliberations with the class. By the same token, fairness and objectivity for the White student is called upon in the interest of attempting to diminish the oppressor/oppressed divide while neutralizing the parameters that the Latino professor has forged in advancing such a study. If racism in its definition includes not only references to assumed biosocial superiority, but also the power to enforce the assumptions, then the Latino professor/White student examination of racism is actually the study of the White students' disease. In any case, the professor is then equipped with both the legitimacy of his/her power as the professor and the knowledge that the study of racism with White students is about how White people have, through racism, victimized their own people. The White student is then certainly placed in a precarious situation.

In my case, the students, in spite of my constant efforts to have them discuss their feelings and concerns with the entire group and

myself, opted to seek comfort back home with the offices of the foreign study program.

The relations of power that have forged the tradition of education
represented a challenge to me and a threat to the group of those
White students having problems with the broader group. Different
factors and assumptions about education fueled the situation. First
there was the assumption that the professor knows and the students
are to receive that knowledge. Such a position implies that the
professor's power as the "holder of knowledge" represents the standard of objective knowing which the students are supposed to inter-
nalize and store. This epistemological construct in education places
both the professor and the students in a defensive situation. Here the
professor is held responsible for the knowing and protection of the
objectivity of knowledge while the students are held responsible for
receiving and replicating knowledge in the same alleged objective
manner. In neither case is the subject a contributor to the creation or/
and recreation of the knowledge experienced in the class. As such, in
a situation where race becomes a factor in the process by which legitimacy is established, the knowledge of the professor is deemed opin-
ionated or biased, making it very difficult for serious critical self-reflection to take place. The defense mechanisms are called forth by the
insistence of the professor that the students recognize their own participation in the reproduction of traditional epistemologies. And in
like manner, the students then become defensive because they are, on
the one hand, not accustomed to such a pedagogy, and on the other
hand, their own racism subverts the possibilities of transcending the
limitations of conventional ways of knowing.

The educational tradition of teacher/student relations of power and
the epistemological constructs of knowledge and meaning which place
the power of knowing in the hands of the teacher, are indeed of significance in our own understanding of how power, and here racism, is
reinforced. Our inability to deconstruct those defense mechanisms in
the interest of developing a democratic dialogical educational situation was indicative of the profundity of their racism and the degree to
which this presented a monumental wall for all of us. The students
afflicted by their racism were stuck, spinning their wheels, intellectually rebounding like a pinball, unable to conceive of the remotest possibility that another way of knowing might be able to help explain a
reality, locked in their own private spaces. I was expected to comfort
them, to resolve their problems.

The offices of the Foreign Study Program at our university were curious about the situation. Yet, their curiosity soon revealed another side. Why had I not secured reconciliation between members of the group? Why was there a wedge in the trust between those White students having problems and the others? What could be done to comfort them and to make peace? The expectation that I as the professor should dictate how people would henceforth "get along" was as absurd as it was paternalistic. The students' racism was reinforced by the actions of the foreign study program's administration. This was probably their first experience with the "other" in a situation where they were not in a position of power. Seeking the reaffirmation that they were in power by turning to the White administration at the Foreign Study Program was exacerbated by the manner with which the administration dealt with the issues. Racism never became a part of the discussions between the administration and the involved White students. The discussions focused on how attitudes needed to change within the entire group.

The Latino students were accused of experiencing "culture shock" (even those who were Mexican-born with life experiences in México). The White students who launched the complaints of alienation from the group and myself, were supported and catered to by the administration. The director of the administration held me responsible for making sure that all students would reconcile their differences. I could not have agreed more. However, I would not interpret this expectation by the administration as an abandonment of the pedagogical responsibility I have to educate; and this meant that reconciliation would be forged out of the dialogical and experiential engagements between members of the group and myself. Furthermore, the allegations by the administration, that there was a need for reconciliation, were never examined. For example, reconciliation regarding what?

Suddenly, the issue of the racism of those concerned White students became a responsibility that all others had to make amends for. I expressed my queries with the problem of holding the Latino and African-American students responsible for comforting anyone in the group. The only position I supported was characterized by a respect for one another and a rigorous critical examination of the positions articulated in the class by everyone, including my own. Such a pedagogical posture was considered inadequate by the White students who sought help from the administration.

The next step for the administration, which by now made it clear to the entire group that it would ally itself with the group of White students, was to make me the focus of attack. In classic style, the administration turned to a different strategy—neutralize the entire group by making the professor the problem. Such a strategy backfired on the administration and only exacerbated the problems faced by all of us.

The majority of the students in the group were Latinas. Of these, the majority were Mexican. The strategy to attack me was interpreted by myself and others in the group as an attempt to: undermine the pedagogy of the entire trip; subvert our own struggles as a group to learn about ourselves and how and why we construct notions of development and "otherness"; undermine the legitimacy of the concerns of the Latina(o) and African-American students that the issue of racism should not be abandoned or covered up, but honestly struggled with; and, however unintentionally, show a blanket support for the persistence of racism.

There was a logic to the strategy sought by the administration. The administration revealed, at least, a minimal belief in the principle of the tyranny of the majority. This is understood by the manner in which it disallowed the students from engaging each other, assuming that the Mexican majority would go against the rest of the group. In this instance, the meaning of what constituted power was determined by how the administration would deal with the Mexican majority, neutralize it, and produce some sort of "peace" within the group—a peace acceptable to the White students. This administrative response infuriated the Latina(o) and African-American students since the legitimacy of their experiences and pedagogical struggles had been violated.

Additionally, there was the expectation that I would somehow accept the administration's position to offset the dynamics of the issue by requesting that we just "all get along" (what I call the Rodney King thing). Again, the professor is seen as the party responsible for establishing equilibrium. But, that was impossible for me, as the matter was not one of equilibrium, but about a larger pedagogical and human reality—the need to dialogue and transform all of ourselves in the process. While such a pedagogical posture is all-too-accepted in much of the literature and rhetoric advanced by so many of us, and while actualizing such a principle is difficult, it must still be invoked in order for the perpetrator of racism to shake free of it. The presence of racism discloses the hypocrisy, fear, and contempt that the racist has of being free. Freedom here is not just the freedom experienced by the victim of racism but by the racist transformed. In such a situation, as Erich Fromm reminds us in *Escape from Freedom*, the person has no need more urgent than to seek something or someone to whom it can surrender itself, wherein that wonder of (but burden of) freedom that he, poor creature, had the disgrace of being born with can be himself/ herself freed of.

Unfortunately, the administration of the Foreign Study Program only reinforced its own fears and racism by straitjacketing the potential for these White students, and for that matter all of us, to engage in a transformative educational experience. The requirements of stability, the status quo, neutrality, and the ignorance of fear cast its veil over the potentiality of development of identity.

The silence I experienced at the poolside at Uxmal continued to haunt me. It was not about a quiet peace. Rather, it was about perseverance. I remember looking into the eyes of many indigenous persons in México and meeting with a kind of relaxed wisdom. I would come to understand that the quiet at Uxmal was not about quietude, but about observation and deliberations. I remember being told as a young practitioner of boxing that if I fought with the anger born out of fear of the opponent, that I would lose the fight because I was not in control of my fight plan. Fighting out of hatred only undermines one's better judgment. I was angered by what had happened during the quarter in México. I felt deceived, betrayed, and violated by the racism exemplified in the actions of the group of White students and the university's administration. Yet I was clear in my conscience and that overrode much of the distress. My greater pedagogical concern was for the educational future of the students.

I have often wondered why so much of what is said about racism comes from the discursive activities of African-Americans and other persons of color, and so little is written or discussed by Whites about this sickness that limits and destroys their potential as humans. I often wonder whether some White people actually think that we don't get what is happening. Do they actually think we are incapable of reading their subtlest actions and words? Have they been so jaded by their inexhaustible efforts to oppress, that their own capacity to create has been slowly anesthetized, and so anesthetized their sense that others feel, think, and fight back against their oppression? And so important to me as an educator, how and where do we draw the lines between what is pedagogically transformative and what is actually a reinforcement of this disease called racism?

A pedagogy against racism is a pedagogy for the rehumanization of human experiences. Such a pedagogy, however, is not about White students. It is about all students and their teachers, and because racism is relational, I must struggle to understand my position in the equation. The victims of racism are not, by virtue of such a position, licensed to violate the same principles that inform their struggles for a healthy community of learning. Where the lines of respect are drawn is a fundamental question to the study and work against racism. Unfortunately, for too many of us, issues of racism are resolved by merely relinquishing bits of power during moments of political expediency. This is not transformation. The White students in the group were not challenged by the administration's placations. The Latina(o) and African-American students were also stripped of the possibility to grow and understand themselves in a broader context. The politics of fear born of the bowels of racism drove the White students into the same state of anxiety and irrationality that fueled the administrative response to neutralize and seek "reconciliation." While much good was gained from the experience, much of the same racist logic was reinforced. As for me, I continue to believe in the power of dialogue as I continue to believe that the racist will only be freed when the victim frees herself.

Chapter 2

I Don't Do Dis Here Dat Dere: A Subtext of Authority in Teaching and Learning

Sandra Jackson

I have flashbacks to earlier disjunctures, black/white flickerings, like old movies on fragile celluloid—grainy yet stark—to sites of difference and white responses to a Black teacher. I remember in the early 1970s, teaching an advanced placement English literature course. I had spent a lot of time carefully planning the course, locating books and supplementary materials, developing readings both classic [the traditional canon] and contemporary—works by African Americans, Latinas/os and women—to create a course which would challenge students intellectually and to prepare them for the rigors of the Advanced Placement exam.

As I remember, after the first two or three meetings of the course all seemed well; however, in subsequent meetings I noted that a number of White students were no longer attending my class. I inquired, seeking out counselors to ascertain what was going on. Clearly and plainly, several White parents had requested that their daughters and/or sons drop my class and be transfered to another teacher's course. Given that I was the only Black teacher teaching advanced placement English in the department, this meant that they were transfering them to a White teacher's class. Reasons given: concern about whether I was qualified to teach their children what they needed to know to score high on the college admissions and advanced placement exam, and thereby not have to take introductory literature and English courses, and get into the universities and colleges of their choice.

These concerns reverberate in my mind much like strident echoes of those very issues articulated by students in Patricia Williams's course on legal theory (*Alchemy of Race and Rights*) who in reaction to her pedagogy of linking theory with lived experience, strongly resisted and resented what they thought would not prepare them effectively for their law school exams. I recreate in my mind remarks which must have been voiced: Is she qualified? Isn't she a bit young? Some of the books she has included are nontraditional—will my child be prepared for exams? Does she write, speak articulately? Can she teach my child? You know, while this integration stuff is fine, I don't want to experiment with the education of my own children. I must confess that these are imaginings constructed from snippets of conversations I've overheard; none stated to me directly. You know, I might have taken these remarks the wrong way. . . .

I've often mused to myself that I've always been aware of a duplicitous standard. I majored in English and thus am steeped in the western tradition of having had to master Chaucer, Milton, Shakespeare, Byron, Keats and Shelley, the various genres, and the periodization of the poetic, dramatic, expository, the novel and short-story canons—a graduate from one of the top ten universities in the nation. Nonetheless, my qualifications had been questioned by parents who were White and by teachers who were White, many of whom had not been back to the university to take courses for many years. Yet my credentials, intellect, knowledge, and abilities were suspect.

Approximately twenty years later, I had a sense of déjà vu—transported back in time to that very same space, place: while the scenery had changed, and the setting, characters, and lighting were different, I was nevertheless *there* again. I had accompanied a graduate class of students to a school where they were placed for clinical experiences, providing them with opportunities to observe high school classes, work with teachers and students, and teach or tutor. I believe that the incident occurred during the third or fourth week of a ten-week term. I had returned essays to students and had reminded them to read my comments, clearly review the guidelines, and then make an appointment to see me during office hours if they wanted to discuss their papers with me. It was a standard practice in my course, to conference periodically with students about their work.

This particular class, which met in the evenings on Wednesdays, had its clinical experience on Thursdays. Periodically, we as a group met with the site coordinator along with some of the participating teachers, to discuss issues related to student experiences in various classrooms. On a particular Thursday, while we were convened and

waiting for the coordinator to arrive, I made a number of announce-
ments and then suggested that quiet conversations continue until the
coordinator arrived. One of my students a self-identified A student,
White and middle-class, commuting from the suburbs, approached
the table where I was sitting and told me regarding the papers which
I had returned, that she was "not happy with her grade" and wanted
to discuss her paper with me. She, visibly upset, indeed angry, had
spoken curtly to me. In that moment something yanked me back to
that earlier experience wherein my competence, knowledge, and ability as a teacher were questioned. To say that I was livid, White-hot
would be an understatement.

As I reconstruct this interchange in my mind, I remember telling
her that I would certainly be willing to meet with her and discuss her
paper. And I added in a firm low tone, that since we were both students of English, I would speak to her from within our discipline and
that I first wanted to clarify something to her: that I was not concerned about happiness, that education was not about happiness and
that she should know that when I read and respond to student papers,
my responses were not made on the basis of whether or not I was
happy with them, but rather that I judged papers according to the
degree to which they followed directions, and the quality of the development and treatment of issues and ideas addressed. Happiness was
irrelevant. I then reminded her—I am certain in a tone which mirrored
hers to me—"Before we meet, it will be important that you revisit the
guidelines, and read my comments in preparation for our meeting."
We then set a date for our conference. Having said this to her, I remember holding my gaze, so that she would see and feel the fire.

Some background: on the previous two papers this same student
had made visible grimaces when her papers had been returned. She
had gotten a B+ and a B. I, having observed this, had already made a
copy of the most recent paper now in question. Having intuited something, I had decided to keep a record. This the same student had told
me before that she was an honors student and that in previous English
classes she had gotten straight As. (And this was not even an English
class; it was a course on professional practice in secondary education). This turned out not to be the case. She had significantly exag-
gerated her academic record.

When the time came for our conference, she did not show up. Neither did she call or leave a message. Before leaving my office at the
conclusion of the time set aside for office hours, I decided to call her

and inquire, offering to reschedule at the most convenient time for both of us in the near future. She was quite apologetic, offered an explanation about a hectic day, and having just forgotten about our meeting. To myself, I thought, how odd; she had been so anxious to confront me and settle this matter and yet had not followed through.

Ideas, strong feelings, ran, somersaulted, danced, did cartwheels in my mind. Avoidance? Second thoughts? Cold feet? Denial? Flashbacks. Here we go again: How can a Black professor, regardless that she is another woman, dare correct, grade my paper and give me less than an A? Surely she is misguided and has made a mistake.

White heat. I decided then to make this an occasion for most *serious business*—as articulated within my community of folks. I decided at that moment to commit to paper my comments and editorial remarks regarding her essay. The result, two single-spaced pages of commentary, margin to margin, justified. I reread the paper and made additional notes to myself. I still simmered. I also wrestled with myself in deciding to go into a mode contrary to my philosophical beliefs: that student-teacher relationships should not be adversarial, that they should be grounded in mutual respect, that there should be open exchange, and that differences and tensions, while uncomfortable, are part of the teaching-learning process. I also resented the fact that to correct her vision regarding my ability to evaluate her written work, I felt it necessary to demonstrate my authority in a manner calculated to not only educate but also intimidate. I did not like being in that space. I found myself between the Scylla of appealing to reason in the context of unreason regarding my personhood and professional qualifications, and the Charybdis of authority and power swiftly executed. This contradicted my commitment to a caring and nurturing pedagogy.

We met about two weeks later, the earliest she could come. I remember greeting her, inviting her to sit next to my desk. I shared with her how the meeting would be conducted: we would review the assignment first and the guidelines, clarifying requirements and key ingredients as well as expectations; we would then discuss her concerns and questions; I would then share with her my remarks which I had typed out; and we would then proceed from there. She listened. I asked if she understood and then invited her to express her concerns.

Her comments focused upon asking specific questions and remarks in response to my editorial comments in the margins. She stated that she had spent a lot of time on this assignment and that it did not have a lot of serious grammatical errors. Therefore she thought that the paper deserved a higher grade. Before articulating my comments, I highlighted key ingredients of the assignment, reminding her of the issues of development, organization of ideas, as well as attention to syntax, diction, and grammar, which were also taken into consideration. Then we reread her paper together, line by line, and I explained my remarks and comments. I then shared with her my written comments regarding her paper, specifically delineating in detail a number of issues regarding the need for many of her ideas to have been developed in greater depth, elaborated upon, and the importance of going beyond mere assertion. I do not believe that she had anticipated such thoroughness in either directness nor specificity, all couched in the language of English composition discourse. At that moment it may have become clear to her that I did know what I was talking about and that I had the ability to clearly explain the rationale for the comments as well as justifications for the grade.

The two-page set of remarks which I had prepared were reviewed carefully and I then offered to work with her to improve her writing. Silence. I waited. At that moment, things were changed, apparently. She became more cordial and ostensibly more open. I invited her to talk with me if she thought it helpful regarding subsequent assignments—her planning to develop her essays, the development of ideas through elaboration and detail, as well as usage and syntax. She decided to accept this invitation and we did meet at least a couple of times afterwards. We would discuss, brainstorm, and sharpen the focus, and talk about frameworks for developing ideas and arguments. She would then share with me how she might actually develop her ideas. She would leave with clear ideas about how to write in response to particular assignments. She did not get an A in the class, but I did see improvement in her writing regarding development and sustainment of an argument, more careful attention to syntax and diction—all not reflected in her earlier work. Occasionally, after the class had ended, she would come by to say hello and let me know that she was doing well in her courses. She seemed to have had a sense of accomplishment and I was glad for her.

Each time I think about this incident, and its antecedent, an encounter across a race and class divide, I am reminded of Freire and Shor's discussions (in *A Pedagogy for Liberation*, and in Shor's *Empowering Education*) in which the authors examine the question of teacher authority in teaching and learning; student resistance; teacher responsibility and accountability to model democratic principles; and

making distinction between the exercise of authority and author-
itarianism. The authors are two men, one Brazilian, the other American and Jewish. Much of their discussion centers around student resistance to a liberating education and processes, and a dialogic
education, one in which students are expected to be active participants, assuming responsibility for their own education and not depending upon teachers to give answers and digest information for
them. Yet, having been socialized to be passive, or retreating and with-
drawing into silence so as not to risk exposure, some students would
resist and seek to subvert a pedagogy which had as its sole or principal methodology, that of the lecture, teacher-talk, student note-taking,
rote memorization, and regurgitation. In their book, Freire and Shor
also address issues of patriarchy, sexism, and student responses to
women educators. The issue of race and its intersection with gender
in teaching was not an element in their discussion.

For me, an African American and woman teacher, the racial, and
color divide was broad—with a White student by virtue of her Whiteness presuming that I was not capable of reading her paper and com-
menting with authority of knowledge or credentials. How could I judge
her writing and ability to communicate? After all, I was just a Black
person, unable to appreciate her skill. Though she too was female,
there was no solidarity on the basis of gender. She questioned my
authority in terms of my qualifications, knowledge, and exhibited disbelief that I knew what I was talking about.

Interestingly enough, I have never had such a response from students of color—African-American, Latina/o, Chinese, or Japanese. I
have had some piqued responses from White male students regarding
my comments on their papers. However, their concerns were couched
quite differently: they acknowledged my understanding of English—
syntax, diction, grammar; what they have resisted is my practice of
making specific suggestions regarding precision in word choice and
syntax and not just writing things like "awk" (for awkward word choice
or phrasing) or "vague." For some, this level of specificity has not
been appreciated, even though, when I make suggestions and provide
editorial commentary, I make suggestions in brackets and frame suggested revisions with question remarks as a way of signifying the need
to reconsider diction, connotation, and issues of predication in light of
the specific context in which words and phrases are used. I strive to
honor student voices while at the same time clearly indicating issues
which I believe warrant attention. I know that this is a delicate balance

not easily achieved, especially in courses like mine, which are not English or composition courses.

As a person who has carefully crafted her own vocabulary and the exercise of her own voice, with a particular tenor, regarding resistance to editorial remarks, I also think about my own responses to teachers and their remarks on my papers. Particularly vivid are memories of high school teachers (for me all of whom were White) who, while quite supportive of my work, were at times clearly surprised by the verbal acuity of a Black child of working class parents. My family was one in which everyone was quite literate. My father and mother in particular were avid readers; they, along with my brother and I, went weekly to the library to browse leisurely and check out a number of books each. My brother and I had to learn the word a day from the column in our hometown paper and we had to discuss new words along with issues in the news at the dinner table. While I may have differed with a given teacher's notions about what was appropriate diction, I never questioned their knowledge as English teachers. That was a given. Rudeness and incivility I knew exhibited poor manners and I also knew that such would not endear them to me.

Even when I had talks with my teachers in high school regarding my papers, as a Black child in a White teacher's class, I never raised the matter as one of happiness in terms of responses to grades. I wanted to understand the basis upon which suggestions were made so that I could improve my writing. It never entered my mind to tell one of my high school teachers or university professors that I was not happy about a grade. I had been reared to question things and seek clarification, even when I disagreed sharply. But to be curt and rude were out of the question. In talks with colleagues, I have learned of occasions in which White students, claiming White skin privilege, have challenged teacher authority and behaved in ways patently disrespectful with male and female professors of color. For those who behave in this way and exhibit dismissive attitudes, I am reminded of the persistence of the color line and racial stereotyping of African Americans and others as inferior, inarticulate, and incompetent, whose knowledge and skills are to be questioned. Here I share with you what I call a folk proverb which runs like this: when it comes to competence, it is for Whites to prove that they can't do something and it is for Blacks (and Others) to prove that they *can*.

When I think about this, perhaps it is because when some White students see a Black professor, one who has majored in English and studied composition theory, it just does not register that I do not fit whatever racial stereotype is lodged in their minds about the ability of Black people to be articulate in the standard code. I guess that it never occurs to them that as an individual, I just do not do "dis here dat dere" and that having learned Standard American English as my first language, and having claimed it as a tool, I have also claimed the authority to speak knowledgeably about the intimate workings of the language and have the wherewithal to evaluate them and their use of "their" language in written discourse and insist upon high quality work in my teaching.

This, I guess, is quite disconcerting, having to have one's work assessed and evaluated by someone who has been perceived as an Other with questionable knowledge and skills. With still so few of us in higher education as professors, and therefore limited opportunities for many White students to take classes with us, I guess that it means that stereotypes are not often challenged through lived experiences in the academy, and that as a consequence, it is difficult for one to give up one's stereotypes and overcome the disbelief that someone with short kinky hair, full lips and a gap in her teeth, has mastered and can contend with(in) the written and verbal discourse of American English and hold sway.

I know that my readers will have varied readings of my account and that the interpretations will not be uniform. I am certain that both responses and interpretations regarding the meaning(s) of the event will be raced, gendered, and classed. I make no apology for my subjectivity in the face of assaultive insults, the likes of which many professors of color experience daily. As one who is particular about my own ideolect and the voice I choose to use in written composition, I am fully aware of the tensions involved in working to get students to be precise and to use words appropriate to the contexts which they have constructed, and synchronous with the tone and mood established, while at the same time honoring their own voices, and yet develop the ability to write and speak with authority in formal academic discourse.

Believe me, I do understand. And when I perceive someone attempting to put words in my mouth, cut my vocal chords, or otherwise negate my voice, I, too, question that Other's attempt to change or otherwise mute my voice. This goes for peers who have at times attempted to translate what I have said to others, as if my own words would not do, as well as editors who have their own notions of what is appropriate and effective written discourse.

As I revisit the occasion of responding to a particular student's response to my comments on her written work, I know that getting good grades is important, that getting As for some is necessary for a multitude of reasons, and yet I must remain true to myself and my discipline in insisting upon rigor and clarity of expression. As one who has majored in English and studied composition theory and literary criticism, I do not do "dis here dat dere." I shall not be doing "dis here dat dere." I hope that the ability of professors of color like me will someday not be met with the surprise and astonishment that we speak "good" English and that we write well.

There is a larger universe of issues here: Gail Griffin (*Calling: Essays in Teaching the Mother Tongue*), in recounting issues related to student teacher relationships and the question of power, muses to herself that we must invoke authority in ways other than through our titles: professor, and doctor so and so. bell hooks (*Teaching to Transgress: Education as a Practice of Freedom*) comments upon transcending binary notions of authority, nurturing, and power as if these things are mutually exclusive and necessarily male-defined. Jennifer Gore (*The Struggle for Pedagogies*) argues for educational praxis in teaching and learning in which teachers develop authority with and not authority over students in coauthoring learning communities and inclusive classroom discourse. These women professors and writers speak to me. Likewise, Katheen Weiler (1994, p. 24), in alluding to Cullen and Portugues, speaks to the "need for women to claim authority in a society that denies it to them, [for] the authority and power of the woman feminist teacher is already in question from many of her students, precisely because she is a woman." For women of color, this means that not only is the power of women teachers acknowledged grudgingly, if at all, but also, that the matter is further complicated by issues of race and class. Within the context of the academy wherein the culture of the institution is rife with the dynamics of competition, women professors of color must navigate the nexus of institutional conferral of authority to teachers by virture of their academic preparation and status as academics, and the struggle to teach students who are culturally and ethnically diverse, with identities which are further nuanced by issues of race, gender, class, language, and other dimensions of difference.

As a woman, as an African-American woman, as an African- American woman professor, I see the dynamics of race and gender as well as class in my relationships with students. As I strive to teach in ways which honor their personhood, their voice, and their worldviews, and (co)create with them a learning environment in which one may speak her or his mind and know that one will not be sanctioned through grades, I must also insist upon a reciprocity grounded in respect for me and my personhood. It is one thing to be judged according to demonstrated ability and practice; it is quite another to be judged solely on the basis of the melanin in my skin. I look forward to the day when students enter a classroom or a learning context, see a African-American professor, and expect the same level of competence they would expect from a White professor and not be surprised when they do not hear "dis here dat dere."

Reference List

Gore, Jennifer. 1993. *The Struggle for Pedagogies: Critical and Feminist Perspectives As Regimes of Truth*. New York: Routledge.

Griffin, Gail B. 1992. *Calling: Essays in Teaching in the Mother Tongue*. Pasadena, CA: Trilogy Books.

hooks, bell. 1994. *Teaching to Transgress: Education as a Practice of Freedom*. New York: Routledge.

Shor, Ira and Freire, Paulo. 1987. *A Pedagogy for Liberation: Diaogues on Transforming Education*. Westport: Bergin and Garvey Publishers.

Shor, Ira. 1992. *Empowering Education: Critical Teaching for Social Change*. Chicago: University of Chicago Press.

Weiler, Kathleen. 1994. "Freire and Feminist Pedagogy of Difference." pp. 12–40. In *Politics of Liberation: Paths from Freire*. Eds. Peter McLaren and Colin Lankshear. New York: Routledge.

Williams, Patricia. 1992. *Alchemy of Race and Rights*. Cambridge, MA: Harvard University Press.

Chapter 3

¿Acaso No Soy Maestra Tambien?
(Ain't I a Teacher Too?)

Marisa Alicea

During a guest lecture I was giving about diversity issues in one of my colleague's classes, a white male student shut himself out of the experience. Visibly upset, he sat with his arms crossed. While I talked, he unconsciously or consciously edged his chair away from the conference table until he was up against the classroom wall. As I described how it felt to be one of the few Puerto Rican students in a largely white grammar school, I saw this student through the corner of my eye and was aware of his intensely negative reactions. A few days later the student complained to his instructor about my presentation. He found the examples of alienation I shared with the class trivial. In short, he believed that since I lived in "America" I had to adapt to the "American way." A couple of times after the presentation I ran into this student in the hallway and each time he glared or looked away from me.

* * *

After finishing the first half of a three-hour class where I was discussing issues of race and racism, I gave students a break. As I left the classroom to get something to drink, one student, unaware that I was behind him (I think), said to another, "I can't believe we have to listen to this shit." He did finally realize that I had overheard his comments and appeared horrified. I had noticed earlier in class that he was quiet but didn't appear to be hostile toward the things I was saying. After the break, he did share a few things and seemed more engaged in class activities, but I questioned his motives.

* * *

In a course I teach on education and professional goal-setting and planning, students also learn how to demonstrate prior learning from experience for college credit. In one case, a white male student wrote a paper describing his ability in choreographing dance performances. He explained one situation in which he worked with students in an all-Black high school, referring to his students as "colored" throughout his paper. His essay was particularly troubling for me because he described students as unruly and lacking in discipline and then went on to explain how he had brought discipline and order to the students' dance performance. At first I was uncertain about how I would handle this situation. I later met with the student and explained that the word "colored" was offensive and derogatory, and that he might want to explore the historical context of this word. He politely nodded yes, but did not say anything. In class, I experienced him as a quiet student, so it didn't surprise me that he had little visible reaction to what I had told him. We finished the quarter and never discussed the matter further. As part of our program, students who take the education planning course with me become my advisees and it's my responsibility to work with them until they complete degree requirements. I did not, however, have any contact with this student after the class. Two months after the end of the quarter our undergraduate director informed me that he had requested a change in faculty advisor because he explained that I was too challenging. He requested a white male member of our faculty.

* * *

In thinking about writing this piece, I tried to come up with one story or incident that would represent the challenges I face as a woman of color teaching in a university setting, but no one story emerged as central. Instead many came to mind. The vignettes above illustrate something about how I, as a woman of color, negotiate self, students, and the curriculum in my teaching. At a more fundamental level, the vignettes also show students' skepticism about my right to be in the classroom as a teacher. How do I manage intense feelings about issues of race, gender, and class—my own and those of my students? What pedagogical strategies can I use to engage students? What are the limits I face in attempting to bring all students into the learning process?

Given my passion for teaching as well as knowing what it feels like to shut oneself down in a classroom, I am committed to devising pedagogical strategies that will engage all students. Facing challenges such as those described above, I must always examine my teaching practices without compromising the issues and critical analysis I believe important to present to students. This essay explores the challenges I face as a Puerto Rican woman and person of color teaching courses concerning race, class and gender to primarily adult white students. It communicates my desire to engage all students in liberation education as well as the reality that I may be unable to do so.

My experience as a member of a traditionally marginalized and colonized community initially propelled me into academia. Leaders of the Puerto Rican community where I lived, my teachers of color, and my parents, possessed a strong conviction and instilled in me the belief that education could be a profound strategy of resistance—a "radical space of possibility" (hooks 1994, 12). The belief that education can be an important catalyst not only for individual growth but also for community empowerment defines my professional identity and scholarly work. Although trained in sociology, I see myself as an activist educator/scholar who believes that a broad spectrum of people should claim "knowledge as a field in which we all labor" and that scholarly work can be an important catalyst for improving conditions among oppressed groups (hooks 1994). I understand and believe, as hooks describes, that education can be liberating and that

> to educate as the practice of freedom is a way of teaching that anyone can learn. That the learning process comes easiest to those of us who teach who also believe that there is an aspect of our vocation that is sacred; who believe that our work is not merely to share information but to share in the intellectual and spiritual growth of our students. To teach in a manner that respects and cares for the souls of our students is essential if we are to provide the necessary conditions where learning can most deeply and intimately begin (1994, 13).

It is an "ethic of care" and respect that I believe best captures what I bring to my work as a teacher and advisor. It is my deep sense of care for the intellectual growth of my students that pushes me to continuously and intentionally find ways to work with different types of students.

As a junior high student, I attended one of the first state-funded bilingual programs in the country. In the segregated environment of my bilingual classroom, we had largely Latina teachers, who, like the African-American teachers of the segregated schools of the South, brought an ethic of care to their work. They nurtured our intellectual growth, and as bell hooks writes, taught us "that our devotion to learning, to a life of the mind, was a counter-hegemonic act, a fundamental way to resist" gender, race, and class oppression (hooks 1994). My teachers taught with conviction and with a sense of purpose and mission. In retrospect, it was in these bilingual classrooms that I learned that education was not only about acquiring specific skills and existing information and knowledge, but was also about learning that students/ learners should be viewed as "subjects acting in and on the world, not as passive recipients of information" (Tajeu forthcoming). Education was about creating and integrating knowledge and about entering into a dialogue with a community of thinkers (Barr and Tagg 1995). These early educational experiences created the space where I learned about unity of theory and practice.

Energized by the possibilities of the classroom and given my own teaching philosophy, I am eager to create teaching strategies that will contribute to students' critical awareness of self, institutions, and society. I believe that teachers should serve as catalysts that call everyone to become engaged, to become active participants in learning (hooks 1994). When faced, however, with students who resist after just an hour or two of class, I am challenged and faced with questions. For example, I may enter a classroom prepared to teach courses concerning immigration, ethnicity, and race, but, at times, as students begin to react to this information, strong emotions surface within them. I may or may not be prepared to do the "psychological work" they sometimes require. Even if I am willing to do this work it is not always clear if it would be ethical to encourage students to open up if I do not have the time necessary to help students process their reactions and feelings. How much time do I invest helping resistant white students understand oppression? If I spend too much time with resistant students, I am taking away from the experiences of students of color and other students who are more willing to explore these issues critically.

Thus, faced with resistant students and knowing at the same time what it feels like to be silenced, I find it important to examine my teaching practices again and again, but to do so without compromising the issues and critical analysis I believe are essential. I explore questions concerning the pedagogical strategies I can use so that "all students learn to engage more fully the ideas and issues that seem to have no direct relation to their experience" (hooks 1994, 86). I also realize through these experiences that, while I may want to engage all students and create spaces where they can share knowledge, there is a legacy of problems that make dialogue difficult. I recognize the reality that we in the United States have learned how not to talk about the problems of racism, sexism, and classism.

Even now, as I write this essay, I have a white female student in the course I teach concerning immigration who is troubled by the ideas I am presenting in class. Feeling threatened and attacked by presentations and discussions of the topics of discrimination, race, and immigration, she began one night to cry during class. She openly expressed the source of her frustration and rage, explaining that she felt that others were accusing her of being racist. She could not understand, she explained, why immigrant groups remained so cohesive and unwilling to assimilate into American society. I am both excited about the possibility of engaging with this student and yet concerned that in her rage and frustration she will shut out alternative perspectives for understanding the experiences of immigrants. Again and again, experiences like these and those of other students remind me that teaching is an act of faith. I may not always know the long-term impact of the experiences and content of my courses. Students who now take my classes and who find the ideas I present in class foreign and threatening may later come to understand them and, if not accept them, at least be willing to assess them critically.

The examples I've shared remind me, too, that in most cases I am not aware of how students are responding to the issues of race, gender, and class that I raise in my teaching, nor am I aware of how they experience me. Had I not overheard my student's comment in the second example, I would not have known of his resistance. Only on one occasion has a student openly said: "Why should I believe what you are saying? It is difficult to trust what you are saying because you are a woman of color and I shut down as soon as you start talking. How do I know that you are not being biased?" His openness allowed for a cautious but nonetheless insightful conversation about his and other students' experience. We were able to contextualize his reactions towards me within the very discussions we were having in the classroom about race and gender. We observed that no one really enters a classroom free of biases and that we were less likely to question the validity of someone with whom we agree and who shares our own perspective. This student's openness is rare. I suspect that other students have felt the same way but have not felt safe enough to risk and articulate their feelings.

My experiences in teaching courses about diversity issues are further complicated by the fact that I teach in a nontraditional adult education program. Traditionally, individualistic and cognitive-psychological paradigms have dominated adult education. The individualized nature of adult education programs and their strong ties to business complicate my efforts to engage students in critical analysis where students are asked to question our institutions. Hart explains:

> The adult education enterprise defines 'competent' primarily in terms which reflect a narrowly instrumental as well as starkly individualistic approach. Since the overall social, political, and cultural context is entirely taken for granted, to be competent therefore either means merely to function within this pregiven context, that is, if one is placed at the lower ranks of the social hierarchy, or to 'make it' by climbing the ladder towards individual success. This notion of competence is undergirded by the ideology of economic growth and competitiveness, an ideology which never appears to be worthy of questioning. Training and education are therefore presented as politically neutral process which are self-evidently oriented towards individual success and overall economic growth (1992, 9).

Designed to meet the needs of business and to promote personal development, many adult education programs diminish the room necessary to critically examine institutional racism and structural determinants of gender, race, and class discrimination.

In the program in which I teach, we highly value experiential learning. Students have the opportunity to earn college credit from work and life-learning experiences. In both our undergraduate and graduate programs, students learn how to assess their learning from experience and to provide evidence of what they have learned through their experiences. Self-directed and lifelong learning are also key components of our curriculum. The core requirements of our program include courses that enhance students' skills and abilities to be self-directed and lifelong learners. As part of the individualized nature of our program, students have the opportunity to design, within boundaries, their own curriculum, especially in the area of their concentration. We encourage students to offer their input and suggestions and we see ourselves as co-learners with them. We tell students that we value their experiences and that through a process of prior learning assessment, they can validate those experiences that involve college-level learning.

I share many of these values and the school's goals of promoting self-directed and lifelong learners. In the classroom and as an advisor, I actively encourage students to reflect on their experiences and teach them skills that will help them to articulate what they have learned from these experiences. My own philosophies of teaching stem from my experiences as a grammar school, high school and college student. In each place, teachers and administrators consistently ignored and in many cases denounced who I was and what I brought to the classroom. In college, administrators thwarted my attempts to develop independent learning studies and internships that would validate my experiences and enhance my knowledge in areas concerning Latino studies, race, ethnicity, and class.

Out of my experiences, I developed a belief that students' experiences had to be integrated into the classroom environment and that learning, not teaching, had to be at the center of what I do with students. As an instructor and advisor, I start the teaching process informed partly by the students' knowledge, experience, and needs and not by imposing my expertise or investing in the "banking" system where education "becomes an act of depositing, in which the students are the depositories and the teacher is the depositor (Freire 1970, 58). Instead, I look to engage students' experiences and their assumptions based on lived experiences; I try to understand how students perceive and understand the world and specific aspects of it.

The strong value we place on individualized, experiential and self-directed learning at my school, as well as my own philosophies about teaching, however, can be problematic when teaching courses about racism, sexism, and other multicultural issues. Students enter the classroom expecting that their experiences will be valued and validated—accepted as is, if you will—but not challenged. Consistently, when I teach courses on diversity issues, some students complain that I don't consider their experiences, a perplexing reaction because throughout the course I do, in fact, ask students to explore their experiences and question what they have learned from them. I also challenge students to consider what Dewey (1938) calls "miseducative" experiences—experiences that have "the effect of arresting or distorting the growth of further experience." In addition, the individualistic paradigms many of my students function by also make it difficult to understand systems of oppression and institutionalized discrimination.

I also face the situation where white male students bring to the classroom what bell hooks describes as "an insistence on the authority of experience, one that enables them to feel that anything they have to say is worth hearing, that indeed their ideas and experiences should be the central focus of classroom discussion." They invoke the "authority of experience" to dismiss the perspectives I am trying to present and those of their fellow students (hooks 1994, 84). While I often challenge them to think about the assumptions they are making, I also acknowledge how their experiences can inform and challenge the perspective of others.

Students' resistance to learning about issues concerning social inequality and their skepticism about my right to be in the classroom as their teacher only push me to find varying and creative teaching strategies that will engage students in liberating education. A learning paradigm, not a teaching one, dictates my work with students. My goal is not to "transfer knowledge but to create environments and experiences that bring students to discover and construct knowledge for themselves" (Barr and Tagg 1995).

Trusting that students want to do well, want to learn, and can learn, my goal is to educate for understanding—to help students grasp theories, concepts, principles, and/or skills so that they can "bring them to bear on new problems and situations" (Barr and Tagg 1995), Knowledge consists of students' abilities to construct frameworks with which to understand and act. A learning paradigm demands that I take responsibility together with my students for producing learning by whatever teaching strategies work and that I help students understand the consequences of their learning for the larger society.

Perhaps what is most disturbing to me is not my students' reactions as much as that of my colleagues who question my motives. When I teach courses dealing with "diversity" issues, I sense a great deal of ambivalence and distrust on the part of some of my colleagues. They are concerned that I "have an agenda," that I am trying to impose my values and beliefs on students. They doubt whether I'm letting students bring their experiences into the discussions and fear that I might be silencing them. Not only does this skepticism overlook that all of us bring agendas into the classroom, but it attributes motives that are overdetermined by race. Some peers view me as a Latina interested in imposing my views rather than as an educator committed to devising pedagogical strategies that will challenge and engage all students.

I was once asked by a colleague if I was first an educator or a person of color, a question that, I suspect, stemmed from his belief that if I entered the classroom as a woman of color, I could not possibly be an effective teacher. Of course, in the classroom, I do believe I am foremost a teacher and, as I have indicated, I grapple with many questions about teaching, learning, and students' experience. But who I am as a woman of color, as well as the many other factors that make up my identity, do not stay outside the classroom door. All my experiences, including my identity as a woman of color, inform my teaching and my desire to engage in liberation education. I am a Latina, bringing all my history into the classroom—just as all my students bring theirs—but, as my title insists, I'm a teacher too.

Reference List

Barr, Robert B. and John Tagg. 1995. "From Teaching to Learning: A New Paradigm for Undergraduate Education." *Change*. November/December: 13-25.

Dewey, John. 1973. *The Lived Experience*. Edited by John J. Mcdermott. New York: Putnam's.

Freire, Paulo. 1970. *Pedagogy of the Oppressed*. New York: Continuum.

Hart, Mechthild U. 1992. *Working and Educating for Life: Feminist and International Perspectives on Adult Education*. New York: Routledge.

hooks, bell. 1994. *Teaching to Transgress*. New York: Routledge.

Tajeu, Kathleen. *Personal Philosophy of Education*, 1995, in progress.

Chapter 4

Race, Nationality, Gender, and the Space of the Classroom: Writing a Pedagogical Story

K.E. Supriya

This axis in turn provides the central feature of the colonialist cognitive framework and colonialist literary representation: the manichean allegory—a field of diverse yet interchangeable oppositions between white and black, good and evil, superiority and inferiority, civilization and savagery, intelligence and emotion, rationality and sensuality, self and Other. JanMohammed (1985 p. 63)

Where can I go that we might live together? Harold Ramsey (1992 p. 196).

Introduction

In a trenchant and incisive critique of colonialist literature, Abdul JanMohammed provides critical theorists with a critical trope—the Manichean Allegory—for examining the particular ways in which the dominant imagination, as it particularly manifests in colonialist literature about Africa, functions to violently differentiate between self and other. This differentiation takes the particular form of a dichotomous, oppositional, and conflictual relationship between the self and the other where the self consolidates her/his identity through an oppressive relation with the Other. JanMohammed's essay provides a valuable and powerful conceptual framework for examining how my own identity as a professor of color was discursively and materially constructed in both conflictual and cohesive ways along multiple axes of identity—race, gendered nationality, and postcoloniality—in the classroom. More specifically, I first write the story of the "effect of" public construction of my own identity as an "unfair" person/professor of color while teaching a course on communications and cultural identity; a construction which had the more disturbing effect of silencing an African-American woman student in the class. Second, I write a story of the effects of construction of my identity as an "oppressed Third World Woman who found freedom in America," while teaching a course on communications, community, and multiculturalism. Third, I write a story about my class on Orientalism and Post-Orientalism where my students and myself dialogically and collectively constructed ourselves in a mutual cohesive and ethical way as professor and students and seekers of knowledge on the ways in which we may ethically shape our Selves in relation to our Others. In each of these vignettes I call attention to the communicative practices through which such identity constructions were effected, contested, and realized by the subject/agents of communication--my students and myself. I also wish to call attention to the fact that these communicative events occurred during my first year as a faculty member in a private university in Chicago. I will conclude by analyzing the implications of such constructions for the pedagogical practices of professors of color.

Race in the Classroom

In one of the first classes I taught on the subject of the relationship among verbal and nonverbal communication practices and cultural identity, I attempted to provide my students with a broad overview of the practices through which subjects from different cultural groups both within and beyond the borders of the United States of America constructed their cultural identities. The class was organized around the systematic and critical examination of theoretical and empirical literature on cultural groups including African-Americans, Caucasian-Americans, Mexican-Americans, Puerto Ricans, Israeli, Japanese, Chinese, and women from many of these groups. We conceptually and empirically examined verbal practices such as storytelling and *patois* and nonverbal practices such as hairstyles and clothing through which different cultural groups constructed their cultural/national/racial/ethnic/gender/sexual identities. The goals of the class were four-fold. First, to teach students an anti-essentialist theory of identity where students conceptualized cultural identities as constructions through discursive and material social practices. Second, to teach students how to gain an intellectual and ethical understanding of cultural identity in ways that do not reproduce dominant constructions of cultures as an other of the self. Third, to both appreciate the cultural identities of different cultural groups and to raise informed reflective critical questions about the practices and identities constructed by different cultural groups. Fourth, to teach students how to be effective speakers and writers—in short, effective communicators—on the relations between communication and cultural identity. Demographically, the class was predominantly comprised of White male and female students, of whom a few are the focus of the story I am about to tell. There were two Chicana female students and three Asian students.[1] There was one African male student. There was one African-American female student in the class.[2]

I decided to frame the class through Thomas Kochman's book, *Black and White Styles in Conflict* (1981) in which Kochman attempts to examine the differences in the verbal and nonverbal communication practices of Black and White cultures, based on which the author attempts to propose a communicative theory of conflict between Black and White cultures.[3] While I in no way and on no occasion communicated to my students that the book was law I did not concentrate on a critique of the book either (and there were some significant problems with the book) as a consequence of my emphasis on understanding the text as a first step toward understanding our cultural others.[4] Therefore we began to examine the text by focusing on Kochman's analysis of verbal practices both in the classroom and in urban public space. In empirical terms we chronologically examined practices such as argument and debate in the classroom and fighting words, boasting, and bragging in public spaces. It is not uncommon for Kochman to make rather unembellished critiques of the power relations within which African Americans are often positioned in relation and opposition to White culture. For instance, one of the subtitles in a chapter on classroom communications reads "Functionality and Dysfunctionality of Black and White Classroom Modalities" (Kochman 1981, 34). In another chapter on Fighting Words, Kochman makes the following observation in the context of a jury's acquittal of the Black Panthers on the basis that a slogan of resistance to the police was just that—a slogan, fighting words, not violent deeds:

"Clearly the notion that American society is 'culturally pluralistic' is an impotent one if it merely acknowledges that people of different groups have different cultural patterns and perspectives. A culturally pluralistic society must find ways to incorporate these differences into the system, so that they can also influence the formation of social policy, social intervention, and the social interpretation of behavior and events." (Kochman 1981, 62).

The sense of contestation and conflict was immediately evident as soon as we began to discuss the first two chapters on Black and White styles in the classroom. In order to provide a context for the conflict, I shall briefly paraphrase the first chapter on differences in communication styles in the classroom. Kochman observes that typically in his classroom Black students would passionately communicate their positions on particular social issues while White students would communicate in an impersonal style about their positions on particular social issues. In the chapter Kochman provides a philosophical explanation for these differences, emphasizing that within each of these cultures the method of arriving at the truth is significantly different. More specifically as I interpret it, Kochman argues that as a people-centered culture, African Americans communicate in order to arrive at the truth of their dialogic others.[5] The separation between person and idea is not only negated but more importantly refused because such a separation violates the goal of communication which is to arrive at the truth of the other. Kochman argues that contrary to such an epistemology, White culture is more of an idea-centered culture where actors value the separation of ideas from the person on the basis that the disengagement of the body/corporeality from the mind/rationality is critical to arriving at the truth of the idea. Therefore Kochman concludes that such diametrically opposed epistemologies engender differences in communication styles in the classroom and consequently lead to intercultural conflict.

As we first examined these ideas a few White students began to critique Kochman's methods and motives. I frequently heard only these students observe—as I attempted to move through Kochman's involved arguments in each chapter and from one chapter to another—that Kochman's examples were few, took the form of mere personal observations of his own classroom, and were selected by Kochman so that he could critique White culture. Such responses characterized the length of the discussion following both student presentations and my own lecture-questions on the book during the first two class sessions on the book. More specifically, during each of these sessions one male student (usually the same) would typically begin by articulating one of the above-mentioned critiques, and this would be followed by other comments and/or nods of agreement from a few others, which served to engender cold, palpable tension in the classroom. Other students would either remain silent or appear restless or angry. During these tense moments I could not but help look, and an extremely painful act it was, at my African-American female student. Incidentally the student had made a presentation on the first chapter in Kochman's text and in doing so communicated that she had gained many insights from the chapter about cultural differences between Black and White culture in the classroom. I was pained to observe that the student herself looked like she was in great distress. Her facial expression was utterly solemn, serious, sober and her eyes looked heavy with pain. She would frequently look down.

This African-American female student came rather late for the first time in the term to the third class session on Kochman. During this class session we focussed on Boasting and Bragging. Muhammad Ali's discursive practices were central to the focus of the chapter. Following the student presentation I continued to give my own interpretation of other arguments and examples in the chapter. Towards the latter half of the class I began to engage the class, asking them if they could think of examples of such practices. A few students provided examples. I then asked my students if they understood the implications of these communicative differences for understanding the two cultures. Instead I heard the student who would typically begin the critiques comment with vehemence that he found the book to be utterly lacking in any value because of Kochman's constant tendency to critique White culture. The student made particular reference to what he perceived to be Kochman's motives—which were ostensibly to differentiate between Black and White practice of and views about boasting and bragging at the expense of Whites. This time my African-American female student looked as if she were on the brink of tears. We were nearing the end of class. I therefore decided at this juncture to directly address the comment/critique by focussing the discussion on Kochman's voice as a White instructor writing about race relations. I asked the students who were critical of Kochman if their sense of discomfiture with the text was on account of what may on occasion appear as an apology to Black culture. No sooner did I utter the word "apology," when the same student continued to speak with even greater vehemence that he failed to understand why Kochman was trying to apologize for White culture. He concluded his critique with a vocal "This book is not fair to Whites." As he spoke the same few White students nodded in agreement muttering, with some force, words that were inaudible to me. As I stood there immobilized even as I was attempting to formulate a response my African-American female student spoke in a voice that was filled with mixed affective states—pain, rage, alienation "But that is not fair to me. This is one of the few times that an author has been fair to my culture." The class ended with my student's voice resonating with pain.

As a pedagogical story of how a particular dichotomy—fair and unfair—worked to effectively conflictually position me in the classroom as an "unfair" person/professor of color who prescribed a text that unfairly silenced White culture. The violence of such a construction was/is only exceeded by the social and communicative injustice engendered by the silencing of the lone African-American female student in my class.

Nationality and Gender in the Classroom

In one of my first classes on the relations among communication, community, and multiculturalism, I taught students to examine the communicative construction of community and reflect upon the implications of their research for multiculturalism. Within the space of this classroom, multiculturalism was/is conceptualized as the constitution of communities of difference. Therefore students analyzed the implications of their research on particular communities—both marginalized and other—for constructing a community of difference by reflecting on their vision of a multiculturalist society; how communities may enable the realization of such a community; the particular practices through which such a community/communities may be constructed; and some of conditions for the possibility for the formation, preservation, and continuation of such a community/communities wherein students would bring in particular conceptual insights from particular critical intellectual traditions—including those of poststructuralism, postmodernism, postcolonial and race/ethnic theory, Marxist theory, feminist theory and theories of sexuality—to bear upon their vision of a multicultural community. We examined diverse communities both inside and outside the borders of the United States, including Caucasian-American and French women communities, American and English working-class men and male youth communities, African-American women communities, lesbian communities, Indian immigrant, Brazilian, and Balinese communities. We also examined diverse verbal and nonverbal communicative practices including storytelling, sub-altern counterdiscourse, nicknames, music, performance, and rituals such as the cockfight as vehicles for the construction of community. At the end of the quarter, students completed research papers on communities including those of Pueblo Indians, African-American women, African-American students, Chinese-American women, Lesbians, the Grateful Dead, and Buddhists.

As we worked systematically and almost religiously through various communities, we dialogically and collectively came to the belief that a multicultural community is one where dichotomous, oppositional, and negational ways of constructing others are subversively refused by the members of such a community. We found that communal subjects would instead intellectually and ethically shape themselves in relations to their others by understanding, appreciating, and accepting each other in their multitude of differences into their own spaces so as to constitute a communal space of both, many. Such was the course of the class for the first eight weeks. Most students would participate passionately in the discussion. There were a few students who remained silent.

During the first half of the quarter I had asked my students to formulate their first oral proposals for their final research papers. At this juncture, one of my White American female students approached me with her idea of researching "third world women."[6] Incidentally this was about three weeks after a presentation on an article on domestic violence in America by the same student. When I asked her what her specific focus was going to be, she replied, "See, I read an article the other day on how women are treated in third world countries. I just could not believe some of the things they do to women there. It really made me cry." I suggested that she begin to narrow the focus of the topic, observing that perhaps the topic was too broad. I also emphasized to the student that she needed to think of how this community would inform her conceptualization of multiculturalism. In other words I wished to teach my student—taking great care not to silence her—the intellectual, political, and ethical importance of conceptualizing multiculturalism as a space where particular dichotomies such as first world/liberated women versus third world/oppressed women, were critically interrogated in the project. During the presentation of the oral proposal the student informed the class, which was incidentally predominantly comprised of African-American women, how women from "third world countries" were brutally subjugated by these societies and proceeded to give graphic examples of practices in societies as diverse as Africa and India to support her claim. When I asked the class if there were any questions for the student that would facilitate the student's completion of the project the class remained silent.

In the same class there was another White American woman student who appeared sporadically during the first part of the quarter. The student appeared more frequently towards the latter part of the quarter. She would often remain silent. On occasion she would appear rather hostile.[7] It was the penultimate week of class. We were going to critically examine an article on the Indian immigrant bourgeoisie and the construction of a national community in the context of a social service agency called *Sakhi*, founded by an Indian woman, which provided crisis intervention services to immigrant women who were mostly from India in the context of domestic violence. An older African-American woman student did a brilliant, passionate, and sensitive presentation on the practice and politics of a national community, emphasizing that discourses of nationhood often silenced women and negated their pain. During the critical interpretation of the article, where students are required to both articulate the value of and the insights gained from the article and critique the article, the student emphasized that, while she had gained many insights including the similarities between slavery and colonialism and the racism towards different minority groups, she was somewhat saddened upon reading the article because it made her aware of the pervasiveness of domestic violence against women all over the world. The student then involved the class during the creative class exercise by asking them to reflect upon communities that would enable women. As students discussed this question in groups of three or four, the student presenter returned to her seat which was incidentally near that of the second White American female student who is the focus of this particular vignette. As I asked them about their reflections on the question raised by the student presenter, my African-American woman student continued to observe that she was struck by the similarities between American slavery and British colonialism. The student also observed that she was disturbed by the cultural amnesia of the bourgeoisie Indian immigrant community in America, making reference to the forgotten memories of Indians who were subject to racial degradation both in India and America. She also expressed her compassion for the Indian women on account of their gendered marginalization and cultural alienation in America. At this conversational juncture the White American female student spoke rather vehemently while looking at the student, "But you should not worry." She then turned her gaze towards me and back upon the African-American woman student and continued to speak, "These women are very lucky to be in America. I was told that if we American women go to India we will be seen as sex objects. But it is just the opposite when these women come to America. See they get liberated after coming to America. That could never happen there." She then looked at me and observed that her parents felt that all the problems in America were recent occurrences. She also observed that her parents felt that America used to be a great country which in its golden past never faced the problems of contemporary times.

Postcoloniality and Dialogic Relations between the Self and the Other

One of the most transformative experiences of my life was designing and teaching a special topics class under the rubric of Crosscultural Communication. It was an indeed an intellectually and ethically trans-formative experience. The class was titled "Discourse and Identity: Orientalism and Post-Orientalism." The goals of class were two-fold. First, to critically examine the constructions of cultural groups as Other within Imperial/Colonial/Racist discourses of the West; in other words to examine the racist imagination of the Other. Second, to examine the possibilities for a post-Orientalist discourse of the Other where the Other is not positioned as the negated and derided second term of the violent episteme of the Manichean Allegory, that which determines the relation between the West and the East through the most insidi-ous, dangerous, violent, and naked exercise of power and by relent-lessly visiting the most terrible forms of subjugation and pain upon cultural others. The prescribed course textbook was *Orientalism* (1979) by Edward Said. The class was comprised of seven students, of whom six students remain to this day so dear to my soul and will ever be so. I therefore dedicate this work to them. They include one African-Ameri-can female student, four White American female students, and one White American male student.

During the entire quarter we/I presented, lectured, discussed, de-bated, and collectively and passionately examined the significance of postcolonial theory for understanding the discursive construction of cultural groups including Arabs, Africans, Chinese, Indian women, African-Americans, and *Pachuco* culture as Others, even as we reflected upon how we can contemplate and imagine Others in all their ethical glory and beauty. I spoke as a postcolonial intellectual from the very space of imperialism, colonialism, and slavery with my students. And my students intellectually, spiritually, and ethically spoke both as students and citizens with each other and me about their intellectual analyses of the power-laden relationship between the self and the Other; through intellectual, aesthetic, and ethical discourses about the other; and about their ethical commitment to both discursively and corporeally resist such a form of power and more importantly to work with compassion and care towards creating a world where we can all be treated and treat each other in accordance with what may be conceptualized as the Vincentian ethos of religious personalism—with human dignity.

Conclusion

I conclude by examining the implications of my historically specific narrative—about how the intersections of race, nationality, gender, and postcoloniality both complicated and illuminated my relationships with my students—for postcolonial intellectuals, intellectuals of color, so that we may forge intellectual connections and bonds as a community of intellectuals, scholars, professors, and teachers whose intellectual prowess and ethical integrity is and can only be understood by those who are also our community—the community of the Enlightened and the Good. Let us always speak up for our own self-worth. Let us continue to "talk back" against the unworthy. Let us continue to strive towards reaching out, together and in our own ways, at each and every moment, to those who have known the pain of marginality so much, so young—our students who so seek to transform the world from a space of Terror and Trauma for so many into a space of Faith.

Notes

1. I have found the trope "White American" more useful in these particular contexts because of the risk of misrepresentation through labels such as "Caucasian-American," or "Anglo-Saxon." Two students identified themselves as "Chicanas" while and after discussion on articles on Chicana culture.

2. The African and African-American students identified themselves as such.

3. The autobiographical account of Kochman, where he explicitly positions himself as a "White instructor," is critical to following the trajectory of this narrative.

4. My students in particular made me attentive to the problems in the book. First, Kochman's methodologies for eliciting the discursive segments that constitute his object of study appear as if they lacked systematic rigor. Second, Kochman often does not provide a theory of communicative cohesion, often leaving students and myself with a disquieting sense of the seeming incommensurableness between these styles. Third, Kochman tends to infinitely expand the signifier "Black" thus obscuring the complexity, richness, and differences within African-American culture. However, as an attempt to seriously investigate into one facet of the racial experience, Kochman's text is in many senses a significant work on a topic whose significance cannot be overemphasized in the contemporary context of race relations.

5. Within my text, Kochman's arguments are inescapably my interpretations.

6. While the students' discourse in class occasionally registered as an Irish ethnic discourse about the self, there were several occasions when the student spoke rather unequivocally that she was an American who unlike the "Mestizas," had only one culture.

7. This was not only evident during a phone conversation when the student requested me to give instructions for an entire assignment on the phone on account of her two 3-hour class consecutive absences and then observed rather curtly that she could not complete the assignment because she had to see the written instructions herself. When I began to emphasize that she needed to complete the assignment she bluntly observed that she would not do so and terminated the conversation. Her hostility was also evident during the next class. As we were about to commence with the class presentation and readings she observed in front of the class in an accusatory tone that I had not given the class any handouts. This was a blatant mischaracterization as I had been regularly distributing handouts and explaining the assignments to students and giving them opportunities to ask questions and clarify doubts. The student then looked extremely hostile as she spoke to herself. Further, a guest lecturer following the lecture made the observation that the student seemed to be in a rage.

Reference List

Anzaldua, Gloria. 1987. *Borderlands/La Frontera: The New Mestiza*. San Francisco: Aunt Lute Press.

Bhattacharjee, Annaya. 1992. "The Habit of Ex-Nomination: Nation, Woman, and the Indian Immigrant Bourgeoisie." *Public Culture*, 5.1: 19–44.

Hocker, Joyce L. & and Wilmot, William W. 1995. *Interpersonal Conflict*. Dubuque: Brown and Benchmark.

hooks, bell. 1989. *Talking Back: Thinking Feminist, Thinking Black*. Boston: South End Press.

JanMohammed, Abdul. 1985. "The Economy of Manichean Allegory: The Function of Racial Difference in Colonialist Literature." *Critical Inquiry*, 12: 57–88.

Kochman, Thomas. 1981. *Black and White Styles in Conflict*. Chicago: University of Chicago Press.

Ramsey, Harold. 1992. "Francis LaFlesche's 'The Song of the Flying Crow' and the Limits of Ethnography." *Boundary 2*, 19.3: 149–180.

Said, Edward. 1979. *Orientalism*. New York: Vintage Press.

Chapter 5

"Leaving Normal": Transcending Normativity Within the Feminist/Women's History Classroom

Gladys M. Jiménez-Muñoz

I am a feminist historian and a teacher. It is a craft born of reflecting on particular pedagogical questions and historical and cultural practices. In this paper I address the importance of decentering whiteness and heterosexism as an integral part of teaching feminist theory and women's history. I see this as necessary because there is a culturally hegemonic tendency to completely ignore how knowledge of identities and cultures is produced, encountered, and dismissed within homogeneous and heterogeneous classrooms. The reflections in this paper are grounded in—but not confined to nor limited by—my experience as a woman of color from the U.S. colony of Puerto Rico and as an assistant professor of women's studies in a small state college since the fall of 1993.

I see the classroom as a political space because I see the classroom as a conflictive place, and this informs my understanding of how knowledge is produced within such spaces. When invoked from the perspectives of historically underrepresented sectors of the population, knowledge becomes an ideologically "explosive" field. Stuart Hall has pointed out (1985, 104–105) that

> as you enter an ideological field and pick out any one nodal representation or idea, you immediately trigger off a whole chain of connotative associations. Ideological representations connote—summon—one another. . . Nor is the terrain of ideology constituted as a field of mutually exclusive and internally self-sustaining discursive chains. They contest one another, often drawing on a common, shared repertoire of concepts, rearticulating and disarticulating them within different systems of difference or equivalence.

This is why I find it necessary to explore a number of fundamental pedagogical issues in the classroom: Is it possible to create a learning environment when teaching history which both enables women's agency and allows the unpopular (i.e., the [hetero]sexist, racist, and class-elit-ist) to surface for scrutiny? How can women's agency be explored when the very categories that allow such a practice ("women") and such theorization ("feminism") are being critically unpacked in terms of race, sexuality, and class? Is it possible to create a pedagogical situation which continually undermines the stability of knowledge even within feminist theory and women's history? How can we promote a conscious climate of permanent decentering, ambiguity, and shifting positions? Can normativity ever be transcended within the Feminist/ Women's History classroom?

Disciplinary History and the Conceptual Framework

Let me begin by examining this last question. The exclusionary prac-tices and internal limitations that have dominated the broad field of Anglo-American Women's Studies—especially Women's History—are grounded in the reliance on a limited number of socially homogeneous founders. The background and the racial, class, and sexual identities and agendas of these "founding mothers" have left their mark on the definitive character of these programs and on the content of Women's Studies and Women's History.

Such circumstances also had negative effects on the very premises of knowledge within this interdisciplinary field. It provided the mate-rial basis for the common-sense supposition—unfortunately, still preva-lent today—that, when one speaks of *Women's* Studies/History in the United States and the British Commonwealth, it is assumed that one is referring to white, middle-class, and presumably straight women. In other words, when the category "women" appears without any quali-fier (that is, when one is referring to "generic" women or women "in general"), one is *naturally* and *obviously* referring to white, middle-class, and presumably straight women (see Hulland Smith 1982, xvii-xxxii). The rest of us, those in the margins, the ones that need a qualifier to identify their specificity and their deviation from the norm and the standard, are the women of color, the ones from the laboring classes, and lesbians and bisexual women in particular (see Lugones 1990, 46–54; Alarcón 1990, 356–369; and Brown 1992, 295–312).

This is why we "other" women and our perspectives rarely ever made it or make it to the center of course bibliographies, book contents, conference topics, research programs, and so on. And, when we do make it, such subject matter usually had to be and continues to be authenticated by some white, middle-class, and presumably straight women—the latter, again, being the ones already established and well-known. Ironically enough, it has been only when these white, middle-class, and presumably straight women started writing and teaching *about* it that the scholarship on non-white, laboring, and/or lesbian or bisexual women began gaining acceptance (see for example, Lerner 1972). Most of the often earlier and more innovative writings *by* women of color, laboring women, and/or lesbians/bisexual women have remained unknown . . . to this very day.

And since the just-mentioned scholarship usually goes unrecognized, then the women of color, laboring women, and/or lesbian/bisexual women who produced these writings—in other words, the potential teachers of such courses and the potential researchers within the field—tended not to meet the qualifications needed to teach in Women's Studies/History programs . . . and so on, round and around, in a vicious circle. Having created the field of Women's Studies/History in their own image, these white, middle-class, and presumably straight women seem to be doing to women of color, laboring women, and/or lesbian/ bisexual women what the white male university administrators did to the founders of the first Women's Studies programs in the beginning.

Histories as Textured Fabrics

To me, history in general and women's history in particular is not a matter of conveying seamless, unilateral, and tidy explanations of phenomena that lay whole and unaltered, hidden and waiting to be discovered; neither is history these phenomena themselves. Rather, all histories are richly textured fabrics depicting the complicated social conditions and events that determine our lives even as we try to change these conditions. Yet the latter cannot be reached intact, complete, and unmodified: it is never outside the variously conflictive meanings through which we attempt to make sense of these conditions and events. Hence, histories have to be woven like any other fabric, each cloth having a different aspect depending on which side one is looking at and depending on the conceptual threads used to construct it (Smith Rosenberg 1989, 101–102; Abu-Lughod 1989, 111–113; Spivak 1989, 270–271).

Consequently, I try to direct the discussions in my Women's History classroom toward seeing any historical text as just another interpretation, yet an interpretation that necessarily involves—though these are mostly ignored—political implications. With Gayatri Chakravorty Spivak, I would say that

> we produce historical narratives and historical explanations by transforming the socius, upon which our production is written into more or less continuous and controllable bits that are readable. How these readings emerge and which ones get sanctioned have political implications on every possible level. (Spivak 1989, 266).

This is why, in the classroom, I have attempted with students to unpack and carry out a critical analysis of the texts simultaneously with an analysis of the historical period under examination. In this sense I have benefited from historian Elsa Barkley Brown's advice on the nonlinear and polyrhythmic character of history and historical research (1988, 9–18).

In women's history, the very notion of *difference* is central to the process of sociohistorical analysis and learning. The construct of difference raises important questions about the problems faced by most women of color in general vis-à-vis historically existent feminism, both as a political movement and as an academic current (see for example Joseph and Lewis 1986; Fox-Genovese 1987, 529–547; Macdonell 1987; Malsom, Mudimbe-Boyi O'Barr, and Nyer 1988; Scott 1988; Barrett 1987). On the one hand, I am referring here to issues that bring to the fore struggles over multicultural voice, agency, community, solidarity, and diversity. But I am also referring to the struggles over the contradictory interconnectedness and racialization/ethnicization of all subject positions—including that of mainstream [white] feminists. As feminist historian Elsa Barkley Brown (1992, 298) has pointed out:

> We need to recognize not only differences but also the relational nature of those differences. . . . White women and women of color not only live different lives but white women live the lives they do in large part because women of color live the ones they do.

These are some of the theories that have guided my research and teaching. But what took place when I tried to put these perspectives into effect within a classroom context—beginning with how these courses were being structured?

Decentering the Center: The Course Design

When I first sat down to design these two undergraduate introductory courses (Gender, Power, and Difference, and U.S. Women and Women's Movements) I confronted one key issue: how could I incorporate the categories of "sexuality" and "race" in a critical way? For example, I did not want to merely add lesbians of color to what would have otherwise been the preexistent content of the course. Such an approach would be analogous to reproducing what white/male perspectives do with the rest of us—women in general and people of color of all kinds— when their masculinism and sexism is called into question: first, they create the "core," the "foundation" of the course and, then, afterwards, they add "women," "Blacks," "Latinas/Latinos," and so on. Rather, I had to question the category of "sexuality" and "race" by challenging the centering of heterosexuality and whiteness from the very initial moments in which the course started being designed. This would mean addressing the category of "sexuality" and "race"—all sexualities and all races—as problematic practices and conflictive lived experiences.

For the purpose of illustrating some of the problems I had in addressing these issues (within the course design), I will initially limit myself to the example of "sexuality." Now then, how could I even begin defining "sexuality" in such a way that students would *both* know what I was referring to *and yet* be forced to rethink the very same assumptions they had about this too-easily recognized topic? More specifically, how could I demedicalize and decriminalize lesbians of color and simultaneously decenter heterosexual women of color vis-à-vis sexuality? How does the compulsory character of heterosexuality inform the identities and practices of all women of color—lesbian or heterosexual? Perhaps by problematizing the historically specific, culturally variable, and socially constructed character of this thing called sexuality I could help students to understand the contentious character of all identity categories.

While designing these two courses I found that "sexuality" was a term that could not be defined without immediately referring to other categories of identity, such as "gender," "class," and "race," among others. All of them reflect anxieties over hybridity, grounded in cultural-bedrock beliefs in the need to safeguard descent, family bloodlines, tradition, authenticity, and so on. I understand these categories—along with the discourses that construct such classifications—to be critical sites where specific subject positions are constituted. However, these subject positions are very porous and have undefined boundaries, all of which reveal numerous subdivisions within what otherwise would seem to be homogenous, stable, and distinct social demarcations and ways of being. For instance, bringing together Clarence Thomas and Anita Hill as "straight" members of the "Black" community simultaneously erases and indicates the explosive tensions within how being "straight" and being "Black" is experienced. Or, to borrow another example from the headlines, Eileen Wornos (the only woman currently on death row) and Newt Gingrich's sister both personify the sign "lesbian" in highly disparate ways—to the point of not being commensurate. In other words, there are sociohistorically and crossculturally multiple and extremely unequal ways of being a "woman," a "man," other, both, or neither. There are many asymmetrical and contextually shifting ways of being "of color," "white," and so on. There is an entire spectrum of unevenly socially acceptable sexual practices which do not necessarily correspond to the prevailing hierarchy of sexual identities, and so on.

What I did in the courses was to analyze and talk about how each author seemed to be defining and using these categories in the various texts being discussed in class. But at the same time, I tried to illustrate how different readings of these texts directly informed the various ways in which these categories were being defined and used. We examined what the readings and/or the readers (myself, the students themselves, other authors) included, excluded, and overlooked depending on how this category-maintenance work operated with each reading practice.

To orient this reflection, I gave the students several sets of questions. Such as: What is the "women's movement" in the United States vis-à-vis women of color? What things, if any, do all women have in common? To what extent have women of color been included or excluded within this movement and how/why? What are the effects of the contradictions that exist between women of different races and within women of color in terms of sexuality? How does all of this affect the traditionally corollary subjectivities of all women in the United States and of women of color in particular: daughter, sister, wife, lover, mother, and so on? How is this affected by what being a woman of color means within the various cultural-national and/or racial communities that these women belong to: being ignored, rejected, subservient, having to wait, having to hide, "being divisive," and so on?

What is the interrelationship and feedback between sexism and heterosexism within the different experiences of women of color from various national-cultural and/or racial groups? Etc.

The Classroom as an Ideologically Explosive Field

Now I will describe what actually happened within the classroom. At its most general level, the principal problem I confronted was having to deal with knowledge itself—any knowledge being defined by placing "experience" as the terrain of truth. Many white heterosexual students tend to dismiss racism and heterosexism by looking at such practices as individual issues and not as institutionalized constructs. If these students have not experienced it, then it doesn't exist. Such students tend to make total abstraction of—and not problematize—what knowledge of social difference might mean in terms of the identity of the knower: themselves vs. others. It is difficult for them to address the contradictory questions of how power circulates as knowledge. Their privileged social positions inform their experiences, which then get translated into a knowledge—theirs—that becomes the sole criteria of *all* knowledge.

Toni Morrison (1989, 12) asks the following question about the Western canon in her article "Unspeakable Things Unspoken: The Afro-American Presence in American Literature":

> What intellectual feats had to be performed by the author or his critic to erase me from a society seething with my presence, and what effect has that performance had on my work? What are the strategies of escape from knowledge?

Let me give you some concrete examples of the conceptual gymnastics, of similar "intellectual feats," the students had to perform to shut out difference.

"Women Are All the Same"

I will call this first example the "Muppet" or "Barney" theory of women's history. Many of my students—and this happens *every* semester—enter the classroom thinking that the object of study in the course is going to be "women's" issues. By this they mean that they expect to concentrate on similarities among women and not on social differences. These are some of the discourses unleashed in order to shut out difference: (1) "I don't care whether women are white or black or green or purple. I'm only concerned with the fact that they are women." In this manner, not only are the collective, socio-historical, and cultural experiences of white women *equated* to that Black women, but two other things happen to these historical-racial distinctions. They are *individuated*: collective inequalities between women are reduced to personal disparities between individuals. Such historical-racial inequalities are also *trivialized*: being "Black" or "white" becomes as socially relevant as being "green" or "purple."

"If I Haven't Heard of It, It Isn't Important"

Secondly, there is the prevailing inclination to call into question the authority of any text not written from a "mainstream" perspective. I have introduced such texts as a way of displacing the existing curriculum, and as a way of addressing identity in more problematic and controversial terms. When I introduced these "unexpected texts"—as students call them (because they have never heard about such literature)—they question the "legitimacy " or "objectivity" of these texts. These students are simultaneously delegitimizing the syllabus—the latter's authors and perspective falling within the category of the "questionable." It is almost as if my very own presence/perspective—as a nontraditional, nonheterosexual Latina professor—is, itself, yet another "unexpected text." Their socially privileged backgrounds/experience only prepared them for Spanish accents that were accommodating, uneducated, and/or at the safe distance of the ghetto (not at the threatening proximity and authority of the classroom professor).

"We're All Ethnics, Aren't We?"

A third, all too common, conceptual gymnastic deployed by many of these students in order to shut off difference is the mechanism Michael Omi and Howard Winant (1986, 14–24) call the "ethnicity paradigm of race." This is the notion that everybody in the United States is an immigrant or the descendant of immigrants, the latter category being understood in reference to the historically European pattern of immigration, particularly during the 1880–1920 period. Such mechanisms enable white students—or anybody else falling into this category—to not have to deal with the differences that other "ethnic" experiences, very different from the white/European one, have represented and continue to represent in the United States.

This is how even those who came across the Bering Strait 20,000 years ago become "just another" group of outlanders who made the journey to North America, with no more and no fewer rights to this land (then or today) than those who came from Europe as of the seventeeth century. Likewise, the descendants of those who involuntarily traversed the Middle Passage, shackled to the holds of slave ships, are not understood as necessarily having a worse chance at a decent education or a job today than those who came aboard the *Mayflower* or who had to go through Ellis Island. This is how "coming to America" from Poland or Italy—a century ago or yesterday—is equated, in terms of one's relationship to a slumlord or to a cop today, with having "America" come to them/us (from the Mexican-American War and the Spanish-American War to the Central American and Mexican civil wars of the past two decades). Recent discussions in my classroom on the rights of welfare mothers or on changing affirmative action legislation strongly suggest that this "ethnicity paradigm" informs many of the difficulties "mainstream" students have in clearly understanding such issues.

"Do We Have to Talk About Gender?"

Fourthly: most of these students are endlessly aggravated by having to do so many readings where the term "lesbian" (of all colors) or issues of "sexuality" constantly surface. A corollary complaint is the frequently raised question: why do I (the professor) have to continue referencing the difference that it makes when the experience being discussed does or does not occur within a heterosexual context? The problem these students seem to have is not that "sex" is being discussed or read about, but that they want to have the "right" (within the classroom) to unproblematically assume, to ignore, and to not have to constantly mention that such "sex" is *heterosex*. As in the case of "whiteness," they seem to be profoundly bothered by having to problematize, or even having to rethink as privileged, something—heterosexuality—which they always understood as being so natural that it scarcely merited having to be particularized or sociohistorically contextualized, much less interrogated.

Such "intellectual feats" seem to inform another common response which usually begins with the phrase, "One of my best friends is . . ." As in the case of the anxieties over hybridity invoked by the issue of racism, most students also resist having to read about, discuss, and, therefore, having to grapple with heterosexism. Within this context, the always-available "one-of-my-friends-who-is-lesbian-or-gay" surfaces not only as an insurance policy against accusations of homophobia, but also as a convenient way of suggesting that "it's okay to move right along to the next topic of discussion because this one is already taken care of." (Given all these straight students who say they have one-lesbian-or-gay-friend, I wonder if that means that there is a handful of lesbians and gays with a lot of straight friends or whether half of the student population maybe isn't so straight after all. . . .)

As with the case of the "Muppet"/"Barney" theory of women's history, these other "escapes from [the] knowledge" of difference, in this case sexual difference, tend to both *trivialize* and *individuate* the experiences of the various sexual identities. Straight students can in this way understand "lesbians" and "gays" as not being any different than "heterosexuals" because practically each and every one of the latter has "one-lesbian-or-gay-friend." At best, this translates as yet another case of "it's a small world, after all . . ." At worst, this means that homophobic violence or anti-lesbian/gay discrimination in housing, jobs, and so on, get reduced to "failures to communicate" between individual people.

Rethinking and Remaking the Classroom Experience

Many of us concerned with multicultural approaches to Women's Studies/Women's History tend to believe that racism and heterosexism are based on a lack of accurate information. We are inclined to think that by rational persuasion our students automatically necessarily will develop a sensitivity towards social difference. The complex and problematic stories summarized above suggest that students are not persuaded as automatically as our expectations would lead us to think.

Nevertheless, there is always a small group of students who tend to shift towards more interesting ways of understanding women's social and historical realities. So far, the outcome in this last respect has been insightful. I found that for most students the use of lesbian texts in the courses was the first time they had encountered readings that examined the lesbian experience. This, in turn, created a space where elements traditionally constructed as female, such as motherhood, could be framed in new and more nuanced ways. Within this alternative pedagogic space, a number of students suddenly realized that being a nonwhite single mother, struggling with socially stifling institutions on a daily basis, was something that could be considerably more complicated if one was simultaneously a lesbian.

On the other hand, I found that while discussing other readings about heterosexual women of color, some of the students began to rethink the degree to which these women were autonomous as sexual beings. Could heterosexual women of color independently practice their sexuality within the sociohistorical and everyday parameters that define their sexual identity? What did/could this mean? How was all of this affected by the national-cultural and/or racial identities intersecting these sexualities?

As discourses, "sexuality," "race," and "gender" operate to position what is spoken and unspoken, and mobilize communities of agreement and disagreement. Within the context of this classroom experience, such an analysis can shed new light on the different and, at times, contradictory ways in which oppression is understood and lived. For example, a number of these students began finding themselves rethinking previously monolithic perspectives on various kinds of oppression. This was specifically the case of those who started grasping the dual character of heterosexual women of color: namely, as simultaneously oppressed (within the dominant parameters of "gender" and "race") and oppressive (within prevailing "sexual" parameters). Problematizing identities in this manner provided a site of learning where issues of "community," "belonging," "voice," "silencing," "representation," and so on could be interrogated and reconceptualized.

These classroom experiences also helped me, as a Latina professor—as well as some students—realize that, just because these different categories (for example, "sexuality," "race," and "gender") intersect and simultaneously inform each other, does not necessarily mean that they are comparable in terms of how they are lived and perceived. Take the example of "race," which seems to be at one extreme. In societies such as the twentieth-century United States, "whiteness" has not been lived as an identity, much less practiced; rather it has been and still is the universal standard of social life in reference to which people of color enact what *they are*. However, even people of color do not practice "colorness" or "nonwhiteness"; instead such categorization falls squarely within the terrain of identity/ being.

At the other extreme lies "sexuality." This time, within heteronormative circumstances in the United States, "sexuality" has been something that people practice, do, perform, carry out, etc. but *not* something they *are* or *have* as a definitive identity. Heterosexuality seems to have been and still is "the name that does not [have to] speak its sex" precisely because it is taken for granted. The latter ontological category (i.e., having a sexual identity), has been and continues to be reserved for those whose sexuality cannot be assumed precisely because it falls outside the boundaries of the norm: certain people *are* "homosexuals," *whereas* everybody else *practices* "sexuality," *does/ has* "sex," and so on.

These are some of the results of my experience in trying to teach about difference differently even as I was simultaneously being interpolated as part and parcel of these differences. I hope this way of examining relations of power can be of some pedagogical use, as well as contribute to alternative ways of conceptualizing and historicizing social differences. All of which raises additional questions about the complex and troubling links between "theory" and "practice": are such distinctions useful, desirable, possible anymore (assuming they ever were)? Likewise, such questions suggest just how complicated it is to separate those two time-honored staples of academia: namely, "research" and "teaching."

And in light of the heated debates between, on the one hand, "materialists," "essentialists," and advocates of "identity politics" and, on the other hand, "poststructuralists" and "cultural theorists," what does this all say about distinguishing "the imagined" from "the real"? Finally, what are the implications of all of this for women of color in academia and/or for lesbian and bisexual scholars, given the prevailing backlashes and social retrenchment both inside and outside the ivory tower? What are the conditions of possibility for alternative pedagogies within these circumstances, particularly for those of us whose authority as professors and scholars is always already suspect?

Notes

1. Stuart Hall, "Signification, Representation, Ideology: Althusser and the Post-Structuralist Debates," *Critical Studies in Mass Communication* 2:2 (1985): 104–105.

2. See, Gloria T. Hull and Barbara Smith, "Introduction: The Politics of Black Women's Studies," in *All the Women Are White, All the Blacks Are Men, But Some of Us Are Brave*, edited by Gloria T. Hull, Patricia Bell Scott, and Barbara Smith (New York: The Feminist Press, CUNY, 1982), xvii–xxxii.

3. See, María Lugones, "Hablando cara a cara/Speaking Face to Face: An Exploration of Ethnocentric Racism, in *Making Face, Making Soul/ Haciendo Caras: Creative and Critical Perspectives by Feminists of Color*, edited by Gloria Anzaldúa (San Francisco: Aunt Lute Books, 1990), 46–54; Norma Alarcón, "The Theoretical Subject(s) of This Bridge Called My Back and Anglo-American Feminism," in *Making Face*, 356–369; Elsa Barkley Brown, "'What Has Happened Here': The Politics of Difference in Women's History and Feminist Politics," in *Feminist Studies*, 18:2 (Summer 1992): 295–312.

4. E.g., Gerda Lerner's anthology, *Black Women in White America* (New York: Pantheon Books, 1972).

5. Carroll Smith-Rosenberg, "The Body Politic," in *Coming to Terms: Feminism, Theory, Politics*, edited by Elizabeth Weed (New York: Routledge, 1989), 101–102; Abu-Lughod, "On the Remaking of History," 111–113; Gayatri Chakravorty Spivak, "Who Claims Alterity?" in *Remaking History*, edited by Barbara Kruger and Phil Mariani (Seattle: Bay Press, 1989), 270–271.

6. Spivak, "Who Claims Alterity?" in *Remaking History*, 269, emphasis in the original.

7. Elsa Barkley Brown, "African-American Women's Quilting: A Framework for Conceptualizing and Teaching African-American Women's History," in *Black Women in America*, edited by Micheline R. Malso, Elizabeth Mudimbe-Boyi, Jean F. O'Barr, and Mary Wyer (Chicago: The University of Chicago Press, 1988), 9–18; "Polyrhythms and Improvisation: Lessons for Women's History," in *History Workshop Journal*, 31 (Spring 1991): 85–90.

8. See for example: Gloria I. Joseph & Jill Lewis, *Common Differences: Conflicts in Black and White Feminist Perspectives* (Boston: South End Press, 1986); Fox-Genovese, Elizabeth, "Culture and Consciousness in the Intellectual History of European Women," in *Signs*, Vol.12, (1987), 529–547; Diane Macdonell, *Theories of Discourse: An Introduction* (Oxford: Basil Blackwell Ltd. 1987); *Black Women in America*, edited by Malson, Mudimbe-Boyi, O'Barr, and Wyer (Chicago: The University of Chicago Press, 1988); Joan Scott, *Women's History: The Emergence of a Field*, paper presented at

SUNY-Binghamton, 1988; Michele Barrett, "Some different meanings of the concept of 'difference': Feminist theory and the concept of ideology," in Elizabeth Messe and Alice Parker (Eds.), *The Difference Within: Feminism and Critical Theory* (Amsterdam: John Benjamins Publishing Company, 1989), 37–48.

9. Barkley Brown, 1992."'What Has Happened Here': The Politics of Difference in Women's History and Feminist Politics," 298.

10. Toni Morrison, "Unspeakable Things Unspoken: The Afro-American Presence in American Literature," *Michigan Quarterly Review* 28:1 (1989): 1–34.

11. *Racial Formation in the United States* (New York: Routledge, 1986), 14–24.

Chapter 6

Identity Negotiation in the Classroom

Xing (Lucy) Lu

I was born and raised in China. Having experienced the turbulence of the Cultural Revolution of the 1960s, I finally got an opportunity to go to college at the age of 22. I chose English as my major as it was my childhood dream to become a translator, helping people who speak different languages to communicate with one another. I never thought that my choice of learning English would not only fulfill my dream of being able to speak another language fluently but also broaden so much my worldview and in some way help transform my cultural identity.

A year after I received my college degree, I went to Australia to do an M.A in Teaching English to Speakers of Other Languages (TESOL). This was the first time that I had left my country and my culture and was made conscious of my cultural identity as a Chinese. Although the Australian experience was very positive and rewarding both culturally and academically, I never consciously thought about the question of broadening and enriching my cultural identity. When I first came to the United States as a Ph.D. student in rhetoric and communication, I once again faced the question of my cultural identity and tried very hard to maintain it by socializing with my Chinese friends, eating Chinese food, and speaking Chinese whenever I could. The question and experience of identity negotiation and transformation did not really come to my consciousness until I started teaching in American colleges as a professor of communication.

First and foremost, a teacher in the classroom must communicate clearly and effectively with students. I do not have trouble doing that, although I speak English with some foreign accent. I believe I was hired based on my academic competence and performance as well as an appreciation of my different cultural background and intercultural communication experiences. However, the first time I entered the classroom, I was made aware of my cultural identity not just by my race and gender, but also by my status as a nonnative speaker of English. Students never openly commented on my accent, but a couple of them did write in their course evaluations that "[the course could be improved] if the instructor spoke English," and "I don't know how a woman who doesn't speak English got a job teaching linguistics." Sometimes, a student would laugh at me in class when I pronounced a word with an accent. When this happened, I was embarrassed and angry. I was embarrassed for losing face in front of my students. I was angry with the student's ethnocentric view of language. Luckily I also have students' comments like: "Some students were extremely ignorant and blatantly rude regarding the professor and Dr. Lu's accent. Considering that her accent in no way affected her teaching of the material, this negative behavior was very uncalled for." Comments like this are comforting and encouraging.

I have mixed feelings about my accent. On one hand, I feel ashamed of not being able to pronounce English exactly the way Americans do. On the other hand, I am proud of my accent as it reveals my identity as a Chinese speaker of English and reminds me of the influence I received from my British teachers and my Australian experience. In addition, I believe that everyone speaks with some accent according to the judgment of another group or individual. Sometimes I wonder if some students' attitude towards my Asian accent reflects their attitude towards Asian culture. In my observation, a person who speaks English with a European accent is more positively received than a person who speaks English with an Asian, African, or South American accent. At any rate, to avoid misunderstanding, I encourage students to ask me for clarification of a word or sentence if they do not understand. In addition, I demonstrate to my students my knowledge in depth and breadth on a subject matter and provide interesting examples of illustration in teaching. I have learned that when I demonstrate knowledge competence and concern for students' learning, I am more likely to be appreciated and accepted.

Cultural identity gives us a sense of self and a frame of reference in our interpretation of our own behaviors and our relationship with others. A person's identity can be manifold as he/she has diverse experience and plays multiple roles in society. In my case, I am a Chinese, a college professor, a woman, a mother, a wife, a colleague, and a friend. According to Collier and Thomas (1988), a particular identity emerges and is experienced in a given context and can have many levels of presentation. More important, identities are formed, negotiated, and challenged in the process of communication and interaction with other people (Goffman 1955, McCall 1976, Ting-Toomey 1986). In the process of instruction that usually lasts a quarter or a semester, cultural identity negotiation between students and teachers becomes an important part of the interactive process of teaching and learning.

In my teaching experiences specifically, as a Chinese woman, I carry with me a cultural identity that is revealed on the surface level through my race, nationality, and accent. At a deeper level, I carry with me the cultural baggage of values, belief systems, and linguistic repertoires in my pedagogy and teaching practices. I received thirteen years of formal education in China and taught English in a Chinese college for four years. From a Chinese perspective, education provides opportunities for spiritual and intellectual growth. One learns social values and moral standards as well as specific knowledge at school. A good student respects the teacher, is well disciplined, and willingly works hard. Once a person enters school, he or she becomes a member of a social family where they make friends with other students and develop a long-term, loyal, and respectful relationship with the teacher. A literal translation of Chinese for teacher is "old master," someone who is a role model and appreciated throughout life.

American students, on the other hand, appear to be heterogeneous in their co-cultural and racial backgrounds but still share more American cultural identity among themselves in their value and belief systems. In my observation, American students tend to look at education as providing opportunities to learn specific skills and a necessary means to get a good job, which is the most valuable asset for an American. They are more active and assertive in class discussions, but seem to show little respect for the teacher as they sometimes come in late or leave the classroom early without giving the teacher an explanation, and do not always greet a teacher who once taught them. They seem to perceive the relationship between the teacher and students as short-term, less personal, and service oriented. In the discussion that follows, I will share my stories and reflections that exemplify the negotiation of these perceptions and cultural differences between myself and my American students in the teaching and learning process. I will develop my account in three phases: Phase one is about challenging and reducing stereotypes through trial and error; phase two centers around the creation of shared meanings through interaction and cultural exchange; phase three discusses relational development at an individual level.

Phase I: Challenging Stereotypes

Cultural identity is not a set of static, never-changing cultural traits. Instead, it is being negotiated and challenged all the time in crosscultural situations. In my teaching experience, the first stage of this identity negotiation process challenges and tests preconceptions and stereotypes students and I have about each other.

One time, a white female student came to me with her paper, which I graded "C" according to my standard. Instead of asking how she could improve her work next time, she challenged me. "Have you ever taught in American universities? Do you know how to grade papers? This is 'A' paper quality, how can you give me a 'C'?" In her tone of voice, I sensed arrogance, rudeness, and even some hostility. I was shocked and felt humiliated by her remarks. But I calmly replied, "Yes, I have taught in American universities, and I know how to grade papers. If you have questions about your paper, let's talk." I asked her to come to my office and went through the paper with her sentence by sentence, paragraph by paragraph. I explained why I took the points off according to the grading criteria I gave the class at the beginning of the quarter. She still insisted that she deserved a better grade than "C." Then I told her other channels she could use for a grade challenge. When she realized that I would not change her grade, she said: "You are yelling at me, I cannot talk to you." I was very angry and my patience was running out at this point. But I did not lose my temper. All I said was "As you please, I am trying to help you, and I did not yell at you." However, I was left thinking, "Would she do this to an American white male professor?"

After this instance, this student became very hostile toward me. She would not return my greetings when I said hello to her. However, I still treated her with respect and professionalism, the same way I related to other students. I also told her what she could do to improve her next paper. When she did well in her group project, I gave her credit for it and praised her for her pursuit of good quality work. Her second paper turned out better than the first one. Gradually over the quarter, her attitude toward me changed from hostility to friendliness.

I was not sure whether this change was genuine or due to her desire for a good grade from this class. But from this story, I learned that I could be an easy target for some ethnocentric and disrespectful students simply because I am a Chinese, a woman, and a nonnative speaker of English. The social stereotypes on race and gender are being carried over to the classroom. I also learned how important it is to keep one's dignity and identity, and to interact with a professional demeanor regardless of race, gender, and class.

At the beginning of each quarter, students get to know me professionally through my teaching. But they do not know me very well culturally and individually. As a result, they will use their stereotypes and prejudice about Asian women to make judgments about me. Once I had a student who was very smart but did not do well in my public speaking class. Toward the end of the semester, she came to interview me for an assignment from another class. She told me that when she heard the class instructor was an Asian woman, she signed up for the class, for she thought she would have an easy time in the class and could easily get an "A." When I asked her why she thought so, she said "Well, you always know that Asian women are soft, submissive, and nonassertive." Then I asked her: "Where did you get this idea? she replied: "Media." I asked: "Is your assumption proved to be true with me in this class?" She said: "No, I was wrong, and now I am paying the price of not studying hard enough for this course."

In other situations, students' assumptions about me as a teacher come from their personal experience. For example, in my intercultural communication class, I asked the class: "Have you ever had an Asian teacher before, and what do you know about Asian teachers?" One student replied: "Asian teachers are tough, deadly serious, and make you do more work." I asked: "Where did you get this impression?" He said he once had an Asian math teacher who was like that. This remark also implied that Asian teachers were boring and had no sense of humor. I could understand such stereotypes, but I also wanted to demonstrate to him that I was serious as well as humorous. I replied with the line from the film *Mary Poppins*: "I am strict, but kind." They all laughed. The same student came to my office a few weeks later telling me that the way I taught this class had changed his image about Asian teachers as inflexible and unapproachable. He shared with me his plans for his life and for the career he was pursuing. I got the impression that he trusted me and also felt relaxed with me at the interpersonal level.

Classroom experience also gives me an opportunity to challenge my own perceptions of American students. From my limited encounters with American undergraduate students when I was a teaching assistant at the University of Oregon, I formed the impression that some American students were undisciplined and disrespectful to their teachers. In the classes I taught, sometimes I had students who came late or left early, and talked with one another while I was lecturing. Coming from an Asian perspective that values education and respects authority, I found it hard to tolerate such kind of behavior. But at the same time, I did not want students to lose face publicly. For me, such a dilemma was not simply an issue of conflict management, but a negotiation of value orientation on face and of different interpretations of respect. With the help of my colleagues, I eventually learned to write rules and classroom policies for students as a mechanism of classroom control.

At the same time, I also learned that the majority of students are respectful, disciplined, and motivated. Through my interactions with students in and out of class, I have learned that many students are working, paying for their own schooling, and some even have a family to take care of. One student I once had is a mother of five children. She was very conscientious, enthusiastic, and intelligent. I admired her courage to come back to school and appreciated her passion for learning. I began to question my own stereotypes in categorizing American students and learned to look at American students individually rather than categorically. I also tried to avoid using my own cultural norms and rules to make judgments of students. For example, I often had one or two students in a quarter who interrupted me while I was lecturing by asking challenging questions. At first I was a little annoyed, because the same type of behavior would be considered very rude in my culture. I soon learned that this kind of student was often more motivated in learning and creative in thinking. Classroom interaction that promotes intellectual engagement and pursuit of knowledge should be encouraged and acknowledged. Now, I give credit for students' helpful "interruption" and tend to have more interactions with those students in and out of class. As a result, I often end up having a better rapport with actively engaged students.

Phase II: Creating Shared Meanings

Over the years of teaching at American institutions, I have learned that reducing stereotypes is only the initial stage of an identity negotiation process. A more meaningful negotiation process requires the creation of shared meanings between students and teachers based on knowledge and appreciation of each other's cultures. Often teachers and students pay more attention to the shared meanings at the professional level on a certain subject over a quarter or semester and overlook the mutual learning and enrichment between them at the cultural level. Actually, a teacher is supposed to be more professional than cultural in academia.

In my case, even though I share with my students the same language system and the same learning environment in the classroom, seemingly at the beginning of the classroom interaction, my students and I do not share very much culturally. However, for the teachers who are considered different because of their race, color, or gender, cultural identity is as significant as the professional identity if not more. Although the professional relationship between the teacher and students seems to prevail, my American students and I are automatically conscious of each other's cultural, ethnic, and national identities. Some students perceive the teacher's cultural identity as valuable for their education. One student wrote in the course evaluation of Asian Communication, "I believe that Lucy was the most important thing to this class. First, she is an Asian. Second, she is a woman. Third, and most of all, she is now living here as an Asian-woman in America. Her thoughts and valuable insight have made us all aware of the cultural, political, & philosophical views of Asians."

For some American students who have never had a foreign teacher before or who have had few encounters with people from other cultures, the understanding and appreciation of other cultures may have to be learned through classroom interactions. For an effective learning process and outcome, some kind of negotiation on identity coordination needs to take place. Such coordination "requires the self and stranger to coordinate their lines of meaning and action in order to engage in communicative synchrony" (Ting-Toomey 1993, 107). Put another way, identity coordination is the cooperation between the interactants in the negotiation and the creation of a shared meaning. This outcome requires the willingness from both sides to learn from each other, and to question one's own frame of mind and modes of thinking. Through identity coordination, students and I learn from each other, create the sphere of "between," and establish empathy and openness to new ideas. However, some teaching strategies are needed to reach this goal.

Storytelling

One of the teaching strategies I use to create shared meanings is storytelling. Coming from different cultural perspectives, my students and I have a great deal to share and to learn from each other. Unlike the traditional teaching method of lecturing on conventional knowledge, storytelling allows the creation of new knowledge derived from our diverse experiences and facilitates cultural sensitivity and pluralistic thinking. My bicultural experience enables me to provide real-life stories that examine the subtleties and nuances of intercultural communication.

For example, I told the following story to my students as an example of cultural differences between China and America: When I first came to the United States, I stayed with my host family for a few days in Eugene, Oregon, before I moved into the university dorm. Every time my host Mom asked me if I would like to drink or eat anything, I would say "no." This is not because I didn't want it, but because of my politeness to the host. In China, if you are a guest in someone's house, the host will not ask you if you want certain food or drink, but just give it to you. Making an offer suggests insincerity; and taking the offer first time indicates greediness. The host is expected to insist on offering a few times, and the guest is expected to say "no" a few times before the guest takes the offer. But here in America when I said "no" to my host Mom for her offer, she never made an offer again. As a result, I often went hungry or thirsty. Eventually, I bought some crackers and drinks in the nearby grocery store for myself. I did not know at the time that my host Mom did not make any further offer because she was respecting my individual choice. My interpretation then was that she didn't really want me to stay in their house.

In addition, I also make opportunities for students to tell their stories. In crosscultural communication class, especially, I ask each student to tell a story to the class of one of their crosscultural experiences. I then put together all their stories and give each student a copy. All these stories serve to legitimize multicultural experiences in an educational setting. Moreover, by sharing our stories, students and I come to a better understanding and appreciation of alternative cultural practices and perspectives.

Experiential Learning

Another strategy I use to create shared meanings is experiential learning. In my Asian Communication class, I took students to several Asian communities in the Chicago area. Students were amazed to see how these communities organize themselves, develop economically, cope with culture shock, and integrate into the American culture yet simultaneously maintain their cultural heritage. Some students, even native Chicagoans, told me they had never been to some of these communities before. One student wrote in the course evaluation, "The field trips provided excellent insight to abstract idealism and [the] course has truly opened my mind to new worlds and new world views." Occasionally, at the end of the class, I would hold an intercultural food sampling party. Students would bring their ethnic food (sometimes prepared by their parents) and share it with the class. I had students tell the cultural significance and preparation procedure of the food through which students shared and learned cultural meanings. Through such cultural exchange and learning of other cultures' history, values, and practices, students and I developed a mutual understanding, a good rapport, and a sense of connection.

Interactions with Individuals

The third strategy I use to create shared meanings is through interactions on an individual basis with students. When I noticed that certain students had particular cultural or academic interests, I encouraged them to talk with me and share these interests. One student was very interested in Japanese culture. He often came to my office hours and had conversations with me about Japanese culture, Chinese culture, and intercultural communication in general. The student had been to some European countries. He shared with me his crosscultural experience. We laughed, reflected, and discussed in greater depth the issues of race and culture. Through such interaction, we created some shared understanding of issues, got to know each other better culturally, and developed a friendship. The student eventually decided to go to Japan for a two-year teaching job after graduation, and now he is back in the United States doing an M.A. in international and intercultural studies. Through similar kinds of informal talks, I have encouraged several students to go on the foreign study program, and they all come back with some degree of revelation and valuable learning experience.

Facework

The final strategy I use to create shared meanings is facework, another dimension in crosscultural communication. In a classroom situation, although students are mostly Americans, they come from different domestic cultures and ethnic backgrounds. Demonstrating a desire to learn about their cultural and ethnic backgrounds provides positive face support and eases the way for cultural acceptance and appreciation. I try to provide opportunities for students to share and be proud of their cultural experience and offer positive feedback to them. As in-class time is mostly devoted to the content material, I often spend after-class time having conversations with students as a means of getting to know their cultural heritage and experience.

However, not all positive face support works effectively in identity negotiation. According to Cupach and Imahori (1993) there is a dialectic tension between positive face and negative face. When students are given a chance to confirm their cultural identity, their "autonomy face is threatened in the sense that the other's identity is 'locked into' the cultural identity, and the other is allowed relatively little freedom to bring other aspects of his or her total identity into the interactions and the relationship" (Cupach and Imahori 1993, 121). Consequently, a face-granting act from the teacher's point of view may be perceived as face-threatening by the student, e.g. praising African American students for their excellence in sports. I learned this the hard way. One time in class after I finished introducing features of African-American vernacular and its difference from Standard American English, I asked an African American student in class to verify if these features were applicable to his speech community. He paused for a while and said: "I don't know." I realized later I might have unconsciously threatened his face by singling him out as a representative for his race rather than treating him as an individual. My question might also have been offensive to him as it could be perceived as stigmatization of African American people as not speaking "proper" English. In general, a teacher's professional qualification is considered most important, but it is equally important for the teacher to know about the domestic cultures and ethnic groups of students as well as the norms and cultural knowledge for appropriate face support.

One time a Chinese-American student came to my office and asked me why she got a "C" for her paper and started weeping. Growing up in a Chinese culture myself, I know how the Chinese care about face. If I had started telling her what was wrong with the paper, she would have felt worse. Instead I gave her a tissue and asked her some other questions about her family and the Chinese American community she grew up in. When she calmed down, I began to explain the paper and showed her how she could improve her work next time. She did a very good job in the next paper. I praised her in class. After that she participated actively in class and sustained a good performance throughout the semester. Now she has graduated with a communication major and is in a graduate school for a degree in occupational therapy. She later told me that the experience she had with me not only helped her improve her school work, but also enhanced her self-esteem and a sense of pride in her cultural heritage.

Phase III: Relational Development

Being a Chinese, my perceptions on teacher-student relationships, expression of emotions, and friendship are influenced by Chinese cultural values and practices. A teacher's role in China is like that of a parent, caring about the total development of a student. A student respects the teacher and keeps contact with the teacher for life. For instance, I still keep contact with my teachers of elementary school, high school, and college. Every time I go back to China, I will visit them and bring them presents. In return, my former teachers give me advice and encouragement on my spiritual well-being, career pursuit, and family matters. In China, a close relationship between the teacher and student is an indication of conformity to cultural values. From a student's perspective, the more strict the teacher is, the more caring the teacher is for his/her growth. There is a total trust of the teacher's morality and competence from the student. I am so amazed by the fact that almost every quarter some American students will come to my office trying to negotiate a grade, which I never witnessed or experienced in my seventeen years of learning and teaching in China. In America, a close relationship between a teacher and students may be considered unprofessional. Teachers and students do not show much concern for each other beyond the academic subjects. A long-term relationship between the teacher and students is quite rare.

My years of teaching in American institutions tell me that the Chinese perceptions and practice of a teacher-student relationship cannot be directly applied here in the United States. However, I believe that a positive and friendly teacher-student relationship can be fostered with sincerity, honesty, and professionalism. I think that when a teacher is perceived and accepted as knowledgeable, humane, and open-minded at the cultural and professional level, a positive relationship with students is more likely to develop. As a quarter or semester goes by, my identity negotiation process enters the third phase, which that is characterized by relational development, likeness in affective domain, and transformation of cultural identities.

In addition to making efforts to establish shared meanings with students at the academic and cultural levels, I also provide students assistance and caring that is beyond the subject I am teaching. When I notice some students showing some academic interests or curiosity beyond the class subject, or I believe that they have potential in their intellectual development in certain areas, I encourage their pursuits and give them the assistance they need. For instance, I offer them information on job opportunities, information about graduate schools, and additional readings on a topic. With the students who have problems with their academic work and who tend to blame the teacher for their poor performance, I demonstrate that I am a good teacher by showing them my good intention, patience, willingness to listen, and helpful feedback. For example, one time a student came to me saying: "I deserve a better grade than "B–" for this paper [a group analysis paper]. I am very worried about my grade." I first tried to encourage her not to be so worried about her grade. Then I went through the paper with her explaining why I gave her "B–" for this paper. I also told her that I would be happy to read her outline and draft for the next paper and to help her do a better job. Before she left, I also calculated for her the total points, which showed that if she continued to study hard, she would definitely get a "B+" and possibly "A–" for this class. Convinced and relieved, she left my office with a big smile and a sincere "Thank you."

Another channel through which students and I get to know each other better is informal after-class interactions. Some students have shown strong interests in my life. I am often asked by students, "It is amazing that you come from China, have been to Australia, and now teach in the United States. How did you do it?" On hearing this, I would take the opportunity to share my personal life and cultural experience with students. Sometimes students come to me sharing with me their interests and problems outside the academic area. I know my job is not counseling or listening to their life stories, but if a student wants to tell me their personal problem, it shows her trust in me and her expectations for some help and advice from me.

I am still carrying with me the Chinese cultural perception of the role of a teacher as an adviser for the total well being of students. One time a student told me that she had been sexually abused, and another time a student told me about her poor relationship with her mother. I tried to comfort them and gave them some advice. This type of inter-action may not be directly related to academic work, but it gives students the opportunity to get to know me personally and individually. Through the exchange at the personal level, a sense of trust and close-ness is established, which help develop a friendly and relaxed relation-ship between students and me. This relational development through academic nurturing and personal exchange brings identity coordina-tion, where shared meanings are created at both the content level in the classroom and the relational level after class. According to Ting-Toomey (1993), this is also the stage of enmeshment or convergence of shared identities in personal interests and values for relationship.

In this process of relational development, a new meaning for one another's cultural identity is created and coordinated. Both students and I come to a new realization of our association and relationship. As a result, understanding and feelings toward each other are devel-oped and strengthened. Students show their fondness and affection toward me by lending me music, videos, books, and articles of com-mon interest, and by sharing their personal lives and future plans with me. They sign up for the classes I teach, keep contact with me after graduation. A couple of students also invited me to their weddings and graduation parties. One time, I entered the classroom to teach and saw "Lucy, we all love you" written on the board. I was so touched and very appreciative of my students' open expression of their affec-tion for me. This sign of closeness usually begins to show toward the end of a quarter. Some true friendship starts to develop even after the quarter is over. I have made a few friends with my American students and we keep in touch by writing to each other. Interesting enough, most of this group of students are females and students of color.

It is not possible to go through this identity negotiation process and achieve the same outcome with all the students, but being able to do so with a few of them is enough to make me happy and proud. I believe, that through this identity negotiation process and outcome, we all, to different degrees, change our perceptions about one an-other culturally, academically, and individually. Our lives have been enriched by the cultural values and individual uniqueness students and I bring to the classroom. Moreover, we have created shared meanings as well as new meanings of our own identity. Given more time and sufficient efforts in developing the relationship within the quarter and after the quarter, an identity transformation for both the teacher and the students could occur; a new identity that is characterized by diversification, creativity, change, and growth (Bateson, 1989). I believe that my students and I have all experienced some of this change and growth through our teaching and learning.

Note

I would like to thank Dr. Barbara Speicher for her valuable insights and careful proofreading of this paper. My appreciation also goes to Dr. Sandra Jackson for her encouragement and assistance in bringing this piece to its final shape.

Reference List

Bateson, C. 1989. *Composing a Life*. New York: Plume.

Collier, M., and Thomas, M. 1988. "Cultural Identity: An Interpretive Perspective." In Y. Y. Kim & W. B. Gudykunst (Eds.), *Theories in Intercultural Communication*, Newbury Park, CA: Sage Publications.

Cupach, W., and Imahori, T. 1993. "Identity Management Theory: Communication Competence in Intercultural Episodes and Relationships." In *Intercultural Communication Competence*, pp. 132–150. R. Wiseman & J. Koester (Eds.), Newbury Park, CA: Sage Publications.

Goffman, E. 1955. "On Face-work." *Psychiatry*, 18: pp. 213–231.

McCall, G. J. 1976. "Communication and Negotiated Identity." *Communication 2*: 173–184.

Ting-Toomey, S. 1986. "Interpersonal Ties in Intergroup Communication." In W. Gudykunst (Ed.). *Intergroup Communication*. (pp. 114–126) London: Edward Arnold.

Ting-Toomey, S. 1993. "Communicative Resourcefulness: An Identity Negotiation Perspective." pp. 72–111. In R. Wiseman and J. Koester (Eds.), *Intercultural Communication Competence*. Newbury Park, CA: Sage Publications.

Chapter 7

"Travelin' a Long Way on a Broken Road"

Stephen Nathan Haymes

"Don't take too much strength to
walk down
a hill, but a lot of strength to
walk up one"

The title for this narrative and the quotation that follows are by
Nathaniel Haymes, my father. These words of wisdom characterize
his life, a life of struggle and pain but a life worth living, to paraphrase
Albert Camus, the Algerian-French existential philosopher. His words
of wisdom have been a source of strength as I have traveled down my
own broken road. My road to higher education has been not a walk
down but a walk up the hill, to borrow my father's metaphor, but I
have had a good time.

My family background might suggest that my being a university
professor with a doctorate from a public ivy university is an accident.
However, what I hope to do in this short autobiographical sketch is to
disrupt the popular wisdom that suggest, that to be "successful" academically one needs a home environment that introduces children to
the cultural capital of the upper and middle classes. Or that children
need a home environment where parents naturally "model" middle-
class behaviors that abet an interest and enthusiasm for learning. This
popular wisdom has even extended itself to being the moral judge of
what defines "family values." Those families that lack home environments that "promote learning through modeling" are described as
"culturally deficient" or "dysfunctional" and the parents irresponsible.
"Good" family values are therefore equated with certain kinds of learn-

ing behaviors and linguistic patterns that get transmitted through appropriate parental role modeling.

According to this point of view, academic success results when "disadvantaged children" are taught the cultural codes and literacies of the mainstream within their home environments by their parents. The popular assumption is that the life worlds of working-class families and the cultural literacies produced out of the circumstances of their lives do not encourage the desire to learn. The home cultures of working-class families are perceived by the mainstream to be impoverished and therefore not conducive to stimulating intellectual or cognitive development. This perspective fails to recognize that intellectual development occurs under both favorable and unfavorable conditions. Dismissed is the intellectual and imaginative sophistication of how working-class people negotiate and deal with adversity in their lives. It is the very hardships in their lives that are the source for their cultural literacies. According to Peter McLaren, "Development in cognition is not something that is passively acquired—people develop cognitively often during attempts to resist—to overcome disadvantageous circumstances" (1994, 26). The cultural literacies of my family provided an alternative set of values that were influential in my learning to negotiate and become a professor in a predominantly white university.

Since I was born into a black working-class family, my parents had little or no time to spend "modeling" appropriate learning behaviors. To make ends meet, my father worked full-time in the military during the day; in the evening he was a janitor, and on the weekend he worked at a carwash or did lawn-care work. Similarly, my mother was a full-time homemaker during the day but four to five days of the week in the evening she worked part-time as a waitress until midnight. When my sister Cheryl and I became old enough, ten and eleven years of age, we were expected to babysit our four younger siblings while my parents worked their part-time evening jobs. Together my sister and I were responsible for serving dinner (my mother prepared dinner before going to work), washing dishes, and bathing and getting to bed our younger siblings. This generally meant little time for homework or if there was time we were too tired; consequently our homework was often incomplete when returning to school the following day. Also, when returning home from their evening jobs, my parents were usually too late or too exhausted to supervise us with our homework. It was not that my parents did not value education but that they were overwhelmed with ensuring that their children had food, clothing, and shelter.

Education was valuable to the extent that it provided opportunities for material survival and security. My mother and father believed that to have the basic material necessities of life meant potentially more opportunities to maneuver around or confront the indignities of white racism. While it might appear that my mother and father reduced education to pragmatic concerns of material survival, this was simply not the case. There were other values that were as significant, or even of more value, than formal education; these basic values guided their more pragmatic concerns regarding their children's education. Their principal value was that their children be able to live a life tenaciously and with dignity. It was the importance of dignity as a black person that influenced and shaped my becoming a black intellectual, and eventually a professor. The worthiness of education was measured by its contribution to their children's self-dignity and self-respect in an anti-black world. However, for my parents, black self-dignity and perseverance in a white supremacist culture that dehumanizes black people could only be achieved if blacks create opportunities to exercise control over their lives.

Even though my mother and father managed to eke out a modestly comfortable life for their family, my parents understood that the uncertainty or precariousness of black life in a racist society meant no guarantees for blacks. They worried that economically they would not be able to pass on to their children the modest but comfortable life they provided them while growing up. Their worst fear was that their children could possibly live their adult lives materially disadvantaged. This was not a moral judgment about being poor, because both my parents grew up disadvantaged economically, particularly my father. My parents believed it is a lot more difficult, though not impossible, for someone who is not only poor but also black to evade the intrusive control by whites of their lives. This was particularly a concern for my mother and father given the nature of white racism in the South where they grew up.

My father, Nathaniel Haymes, grew up in the racially segregated city of Danville, Virginia. He did not finish high school, but received his high school equivalency while in the United States Army during the Korean War. He entered the army at the age of seventeen, like many young black men growing up in the racially segregated South. His father, Walter, earned twenty dollars a week as a blacksmith at a coal yard, and his mother, Kallie, thirty-five cents an hour as a factory worker in a tobacco processing plant. My father and his five siblings, none of whom completed high school or an equivalent, along with both parents, lived in extreme poverty.

The black community of Danville was geographically confined to the fairgrounds neighborhood. The small house my father's parents rented from a white landlord had no indoor running water, kitchen sink and bathroom, which was not the case for whites. Also, six children and two adults shared one bedroom, a living room transformed into a bedroom, and kitchen. These living conditions were the norm for black families in Danville. In defiance of these circumstances, my father maintains that his family and other black families in the fairgrounds neighborhood still lived a "good life because there was a lot of love." "Because people took care of each other, black people were able to be happy regardless of racism and the hardships it created in their everyday lives, he contends. He also attributes the low black suicide rate at that time to the caring relationships fostered by black people. My father also noted that the close-knit relationships formed were ironically facilitated by the geographical separation between blacks and whites. It provided a buffer from the intrusion of white people into the everyday lives of blacks.

Racial mistreatment in the segregated South also meant that to survive, black people often had no other choice but to make a living doing some of the most dangerous, backbreaking low paid work. To survive, many poor southern black families had no other choice but to have their children work in oppressive work conditions; this was often alongside them, whether that be factory or agricultural work. Also, it was through the institution of work that white supremacy in the South exercised its control and regulation of the black body and spirit. Much of my father's life, because of his experiences in the racially segregated South, has involved a determination, or outright refusal, to be controlled by whites. That experience taught him how to navigate in ways that secured for him a sense of independence from white surveillance and control. Instead of contributing to the family income by working in a factory, my father, at the age of ten, rummaged garbage dumps daily for scrap metal and empty glass bottles to sell. And at twelve years old, he owned a corner grocery store that later burned down. At age sixteen he migrated alone to New York City to work for his uncle, who owned a bar and grill in Harlem. While in New York City, on his seventeenth birthday, he claimed to be eighteen to enlist in the army. Twenty-two years later, serving three tours of war duty, once in Korea and twice in Vietnam, he retired at the age of thirty-nine as a first sergeant.

My mother, Bernice Everrett, the youngest of twelve children, was born in a small rural town in the segregated South called Newsom, Virginia. Her parents, John and Eda Everrett, eventually purchased the land they sharecropped and became peanut farmers. She graduated from an all-black high school where she and other young black women were trained in home economics. Like many young black women of her generation, my mother was trained in high school to do domestic work for middle-class southern white families. White men would regularly solicit my grandfather for one of his daughters to do domestic work in their homes. His response was absolutely no, that his daughters would never clean the home of a white man. What probably encouraged my grandfather to respond this way was that it was not uncommon for young black girls and women doing domestic work for white families to be repeatedly raped and sexually abused by white men. For my grandfather to respond so directly required a great deal of courage in that it was not uncommon for a mob of white men to retaliate with physical violence. My grandfather could have easily been accused by whites of not knowing his place as a "nigger" and therefore in need of a physical beating, or death by lynching. My mother recalls stories of my grandfather defiantly refusing to obey "white only" signs. One particular story was when my grandfather refused to pay for the hamburgers, fries, and soda he had ordered for himself, my grandmother, and my mother, who was a young girl, because the white storeowner refused to let my grandmother use the bathroom. My mother remembers after this incident, how she and her young female friends would order food at a white-owned diner, and if they were refused a seat at the "white only" counter, they would return the food and refuse to pay.

The source of my family values derives from the generations of folk in my family who witnessed and graciously endured with dignity the experiences of antiblack racism in the segregated South. Education—thinking, feeling, reading, writing, and dialoguing—became the avenue through which I turned the pain of denigration and disrespect for black life into theory about how to live life. The oral histories told by my parents about their lives and the lives of family members and friends were choreographed to teach lessons about life and how to survive its harshness. It was these oral histories and the cultural literacies they provided about black life that encouraged me eventually to want to make the bridge between home and school cultures. However, it was not until many years after high school that I had the opportunity to bridge these two worlds.

Educated in mixed class, predominately white elementary and secondary schools in Poughkeepsie, New York, I was for a short time placed in special education while in elementary school. I was diagnosed as having a below average IQ. While my father was serving military duty in Vietnam, my mother challenged the accuracy of the diagnosis and requested that I be taken out of special education classes. The school refused and also rejected her demand that I be reassessed by the school psychologists. In response my mother took me to a university educational psychologist who determined that I had a better than average IQ. The reaction of the school was to place me in general education classes and hold me back one grade. Eventually, because of my mother's insistence that I be enrolled in college preparation courses, I was placed into a dual track, taking a combination of college preparation and general education courses. Also, while in this dual track I was encouraged by the high school guidance counselor, who was white, to enroll in vocational education courses and to register in what is known today as a school-to-work program. Incidentally, it was during my senior year, when discussing my career aspirations with the guidance counselor, that I had casually glanced onto the counselor's desk to discover written on a card with my name typed at the top the number sixty. I do not remember the reasons why I was curious, but after school I asked my parents if they knew what was that number on the card. I recall how my mother and father looked at each other with surprise and apprehension on their faces when I had found something they had not wanted me to know until well after I finished high school. My parents repeatedly tell me to this day that they fought the school's diagnosis and recommendations because they knew what their children where capable of and that my mind was not slow. Both continually refer to how as a child I was the one among my siblings who constantly asked questions that they sometimes were unable to answer. They quenched my curiosity about things by buying me a microscope, telescope, and a chemistry and biology set. They thought I was a precocious child in that I would constantly go to the pond, catch frogs, dissect them, identify their internal organs, and try to keep the frogs alive while I performed open heart surgery. And, when *Apollo* landed on the moon I had dreams of being an astronaut. When they bought me my first telescope and I learned by myself to identify planets and star constellations, my nickname at home became "the professor."

After graduating from high school I attended the University of New Mexico in Albuquerque. Like many undergraduates, I was uncertain about what I wanted to study or whether I wanted to go to school at all. My decision to go to college was largely motivated by my wanting to do some traveling, and New Mexico sounded great. I remember being excited about looking at those encyclopedia-like books that listed and described different universities and colleges throughout the country. When looking at the college catalogues my attitude was like that of a tourist seeking a great adventure. While at the University of New Mexico I initially majored as an undergraduate in exercise physiology, in which the university had a national reputation. My reason for majoring in exercise physiology was that to some extent I was familiar with it given that I was a superstar high school track and football athlete. However, I was not very excited about majoring in this area; the principal reason being that my high school senior year as an athlete was filled with much disappointment.

During a high school football awards banquet which my parents and I attended, the only family of color present, I was overlooked for receiving the best running back of the year award. Instead, the award was given to a white teammate whose statistical performance was significantly below mine. This incident made me very disenchanted with athletics. It also raised for me questions about race. I remember feeling as though my black body had been exploited by the team's white coaches. That incident made me recognize that the coaches never gave a damn about my academics or my future. I felt betrayed and wanted to hide because I felt so very naive and embarrassed that I had allowed myself to be reduced to just a body. This made me for the first time consciously acknowledge that I was not prepared academically to attend college. With this came much resentment towards those white teachers and administrators in my elementary and secondary experience who were supposed to prepare me. It was these feelings of self-doubt, anger, and betrayal that I brought with me to New Mexico.

After my first year at the University of New Mexico I dropped out with a below average GPA and enlisted in the United States Army. At a recruitment station in Albuquerque, I enlisted at the age of twenty because it was also something that I was familiar with since it was my father's career. However, when I arrived at Fort Leonardwood, Missouri, for basic training I began to question my decision to enlist. It was the "Iranian crisis" of the late 1970s that caused me to reevaluate the purposes of the U.S. Army and whether I could perform the demands it required of me as a soldier. The events in Tehran caused me to see that I had been duped by the army's popular advertisements that if a young man and women joined the army they could learn a new job skill and also travel. I remember while flying to basic training with other new recruits, who incidentally were mostly men of color, we were confident in our conversations that the army would better prepare us occupationally for civilian life. The hostage standoff in Iran awakened me to the fact that the real purpose of the army was to fight wars. And that most of us new recruits would learn job skills that were not transferable to civilian life, but were only limited to the battlefield.

The bombardment of national news media reports suggested that the Iranian crisis represented a national security threat because it could inspire a regional alliance among Arab countries that could seriously affect the flow of oil to the West. My reaction was that I was not willing to die for oil companies and make some oil executive filthy rich. The emotional atmosphere at basic training camp during this period was one of anxiety for us new recruits. Drill sergeants and company commanders manipulated not only our fears and anxieties about war but fueled those raw emotions by repeatedly announcing that Fort Leonardwood was being placed on combat alert and that we new recruits would be the first to go to battle in Iran. Whether they had intended to or not, many of the new recruits I had befriended became diligent and gung-ho about soldiering and learning the basic skills of combat. However, I found myself resistant to becoming gung-ho and therefore more insistent that I was not going to die to make someone already rich richer. It is at this time that I began to question the military's purposes and connect its reason for being to protecting rich people's economic interests.

The motivation for my questioning and even resistance was a high school senior social studies course elective on the Vietnam War taught from an antiwar perspective. Another student and I invited our fathers, who had served tours of duty in Vietnam. I remember being surprised that my father had many concerns about the United States's involvement in Vietnam. According to my father, the war was "unethical." He said, "it was a politician's war not a war supported by public opinion." Too many people died, and "the richer got richer and the poorer got poorer." Another cause for my not being enthusiastic about serving in the army was its racism. White commissioned and noncommissioned officers took noticeably contemptuous attitudes and actions towards young black enlisted soldiers. And despite the army's rhetoric of equality, black men were disproportionately infantry soldiers, not officers, inmates in the military prisons, reprimanded with money docked from their pay. My personal experiences and observations constantly reminded me of my father's personal stories about racism in the military.

Stationed at Fort Carson in Colorado Springs, Colorado, I decided after two years in the army to legally pursue being honorably discharged as a conscientious objector. While in Colorado Springs I befriended an ex-United States congressman from the East Coast, Bill Durland, who was also a lawyer, peace activist, and director of the Center for Peace and Pacifism. Along with meeting Bill I also became involved with a local white Christian-based activist peace community. It was with this community that I was first introduced to civil disobedience and demonstrations. The demonstrations I participated in while serving in the army were protests against U.S. military spending, and militarism in third world countries, particularly Latin America. Also, I did work in soup kitchens and hospitality houses for the homeless, run also by the local Christian-based peace community.

These involvements provided me the opportunity to participate in reading groups and discussions about social justice. The first time I was placed in police custody while demonstrating was when I instructed eighteen-year-old males in front of the post office not to register for the draft and refused with other demonstrators to vacate the premises. While in custody the local police discovered that I was a soldier stationed at Fort Carson. The military police came and took me into custody and contained me at the military police office on base. I was questioned as to my "subversive activities" and was told that my commanding officer had informed them of my continued resistance to wearing the uniform and participating in war exercises. But interestingly my commanding officer instructed the military police to let me go home. Before this incident, I had shared an article with him from *Sojourner's*, a Christian peace activist publication, in which there was an interview with the Catholic priest who had given communion to the airmen who dropped the atomic bomb on Hiroshima and Nagasaki. In that interview he had explained that after the bombing he could no longer in good faith serve in the military as a chaplain. My intention for giving my commanding officer this article was to have him understand why I disobeyed orders to participate in war exercises. And also to convince him that it was possible for a soldier while in the military to be morally in anguish and compelled to reconsider his military obligation. After taking the article into his office to read he instructed me to go home and that he would respect my wishes not to participate in the war exercises. Also during this time, I had repeatedly written the base commander, a general, expressing to him my moral reservations about continuing to serve in the army.

Months after communicating with the base commander, he had agreed to honor my request that I be given a hearing with respect to my petition to be released from the army as a conscientious objector, with an honorable discharge. In support of my testimony the Catholic priest, who had given communion to the airmen testified at the hearing. Six months after my hearing the United States Army released me as a conscientious objector with an honorable discharge. Also, my case was a landmark case. It was the first case since the end of the Vietnam War of a soldier released as conscientious objector. In addition, my case was the only case ever where a soldier received an administrative hearing and was released as conscientious objector. During the Gulf War soldiers petitioning to be released as conscientious objectors referred to my case; however none were granted an administrative hearing by the military. Since the time of the Gulf War, soldiers requesting to be released as conscientious objectors have had to use the federal courts.

After my release I returned to the University of New Mexico to major in political philosophy and sociology and raised my GPA to 3.6. While there I continued to be involved as a student activist. I was involved in such activities as the university disinvestment in South African campaign, El Salvador and Nicaraguan student solidarity groups, Democratic Socialists of America, the Progressive Student Alliance. I was also the Black studies history month chair who was responsible for bringing the Granadian Ambassador and CLR James to the United Nations. This period for me was a time of much reading and dialoguing with friends, and enrolling in courses that were exciting and relevant to my life. It is this experience that has shaped the nature of my university teaching in which education is not just about striving for knowledge in books, but knowlege about how to live in the world.

Ironically, my experiences from the military ignited my curiosity and enthusiasm for wanting to dedicate my life to eradicating the roots of social injustice. While my elementary and secondary schooling experiences had been an obstacle to my academic development, my arduous life experiences had become the basis for awakening my self-confidence as a thinker and learner. Though my experiences in the military were important for the remaking of myself, it was the values that my parents passed on to me that gave me the strength to "go through storm." My mother's tenacity to confront an all-white school system that repeatedly told her that I would "never be college material" is an example of her strength and self-confidence as a black woman. It is my mother's perseverance and my father's resilience in maintaining his independence as a black man in a white-dominated world that has informed how I negotiate life, and have made possible my eventually becoming an university professor. These "core" values express an intellectual attitude that stands on principle, "tells it like it is" or, as Edward Said states, "tells the truth to power." This is an attitude that does not evade the adversities of life but develops out of this adversity a passion for living life. However, in a culture like the university, dominated by the codes of the middle class, this attitude is often characterized as being "difficult," "uncooperative," or emotional. The quote that follows by David Wellman, a white working-class intellectual, portrays my own thoughts and experiences as a black working-class male in the university:

> I know I am a border person when I realize university culture practices an etiquette that only certain people are taught. It is a class etiquette, gendered as well, and, as I discovered in graduate school, it is learned at the elite colleges where many university professors begin as undergraduates. The working knowledge of this culture is not shared with class outsiders. It is not discussed at career counseling meetings for junior faculty. Being 'too passionate,' we learn, is unacceptable. So is being committed to principles which university insiders call being 'inflexible' or 'unreasonable.' We discover that survival in the academy depends upon learning that it is inappropriate to argue from the heart, or from a position of principle. The appropriate method is to invoke 'empirical evidence,' or remain silent until sufficient 'data' have been collected. Border academics find out that direct talk, 'telling it like it is'—or 'speaking truth to power'—is counterproductive. The delicate language of euphemism and indirectness is the lingua franca. One learns that behavior which would be severely sanctioned on the mean streets of Detroit is acceptable in university settings where it is permissible to destroy someone's career so long as procedures are followed, and confidentiality is maintained. Outsiders soon discover that it is all right to impugn another's honor and integrity so long as it's done cleverly, with humor, and in 'good taste' (1996:38).

Reference List

McLaren, Peter. 1994. *Life in Schools: An Introduction to Critical Pedagogy in Foundations of Education*. New York: Longman.

Wellman, David. 1996. "Red and Black in White America: Discovery Cross-Border Identities and Other Subversive Activities" in *Names We Call Home: Autobiography on Racial Identity*, Becky Thompson and Sangerta Tyagi, Eds. Routledge: New York.

Chapter 8

A Cubana in the Classroom: The Experiences of One Latina in Academia

Maria R. Vidal

Introduction

Mother, wife, Latina, woman, Cuban, daughter, sister, immigrant, American, middle class, an academic. These are all dimensions or aspects of my identity. There is no hierarchy or rank ordering of these dimensions—in fact they really cannot be disentangled. I list them all because they have far-reaching implications for my life in academia. These dimensions of my identity strongly inform and influence what I teach, how I teach, the focus of my scholarship, my relationships with my colleagues, and the service I perform outside of the university.

Who I Am

I was born in Cienfuegos, Cuba, in October 1962, during the eleventh hour of the Missile Crisis. My family resided in Trinidad, a small town to the east, but had made the trip to Cienfuegos for my birth since the doctors had been sent to key sites across the island during the crisis, leaving our small historic town without a physician. Before leaving the hospital and Cienfuegos for home, my parents had a passport photograph taken of me in preparation to depart the country as soon as possible. Nine months later my parents were notified that their petition to leave the country had been granted and that we would have to leave immediately. I embarked on a U.S. Red Cross ship with my parents, sister, and great aunt on that same day. The ship had unloaded

its cargo of donated pharmaceuticals and medical supplies and returned to the U.S. with its new cargo of Cuban passengers. This trip
was not typical. We had come to the U.S. during a time when relatively few Cubans were coming. The first wave of unrestricted immigration was over and it was prior to the freedom flights that brought
thousands more Cubans to the U.S. Interestingly, we arrived on the
Miami shore on July 4, 1963, in the midst of Independence Day celebrations.

My parents had decided to leave the island several years earlier,
following the Cuban revolution of 1959. They did not support the
revolutionary government of Fidel Castro and made an application to
exit Cuba. However, their early efforts were in vain. Their application
went unanswered or was denied, while those of my brothers and newborn sister were granted. Fearing that my brothers might possibly have
no other opportunity to leave, or that should they delay too long they
could reach the age for mandatory military service, my parents sent
them ahead to the United States. In 1961, in their early teens, my
brothers made the 90-mile trip from Cuba to Miami. Many other Cuban youths were also coming to the U.S. under similar circumstances.
In response, the federal government financed the Peter Pan Program,
a full-scale resettlement program for unaccompanied Cuban youth.
After a brief stay in Miami for processing, my brothers were sent to
Lincoln, Nebraska, to live in Cristo Rey, a Catholic residential facility
funded through the Peter Pan Program. They lived there with about
100 other Cuban boys and girls awaiting the arrival of their parents.

Like my brothers before us, we spent a short time in Miami for
processing and followed to Nebraska to join them. We were greeted at
the airport by Father Tuchek, the director of Cristo Rey, and my brothers. Although I have no recollection of this reunion, as a parent I can
imagine the overwhelming emotion that they must have felt. After
leaving the airport, Fr. Tuchek took us to a three-bedroom house that
he had rented and filled with donated second-hand furniture for my
family. In the ensuing weeks he assisted my parents in resettling in
Lincoln.

This new life for my family was vastly different from our previous
life. Both of my parents were college educated, prosperous professionals. My mother was an art instructor at a local college and my
father was an accountant for his father's shipyard, ice plant, and can-
nery. They enjoyed the material and social privilege that came with
their position. They had a stylish historic home facing the town plaza

and membership in the Trinidad society clubs. This lifestyle changed dramatically upon their arrival in the U.S. Our rented house was old, in need of repair, and in a working poor section of town. We got by with the assistance of public aid, food stamps, and Medicaid until my parents were able to secure employment. After a few months my father was able to get a job as a custodian in the city's largest public high school. Shortly after, my mother began cleaning dormitory rooms at the state university. Their new life was initially marked by insecurity, financial struggle, discrimination, and indignities in the work place.

Eventually my father secured a position in a printing company that allowed him to utilize his artistic talent. He had not formally studied art as my mother had, yet he had a tremendous natural gift for drawing, calligraphy, and design. This job allowed my mother to stay home to care for my ailing great aunt and for our family to eventually purchase a modest bungalow in a stable working-class neighborhood. While this job did not provide room for advancement or retirement benefits, it granted him some security, respect, and an avenue for self-expression, so he remained there until his retirement at age 65.

My experience as an immigrant was, of course, very different from that of my parents and older siblings. I don't have memories of being unable to express myself in a language that others could understand. Nor can I recall the feelings of fear, uncertainty, and great risk that characterized my brothers' and parents' passage to the U.S. I did not have to say good-bye to my friends, family, and homeplace. I do have some feelings of longing for my "homeland," but in a way that is very different from my parents and older siblings.

Since I had immigrated at such a young age I learned English and Spanish simultaneously. Spanish was the language of home and English was what I spoke with my neighborhood playmates. By the time I entered school I was completely bilingual. My fluency in English made my transition to school easy, but it also brought tremendous responsibility. By the time I could read and write my older brothers had left the house; one had married and the other had departed for college. My older sister was shy, reluctant to assist my parents in their transactions with the world outside of our family. Thus, I became the translator for my parents. I translated at doctors' offices, at the grocery store, and government offices. I accompanied my father in his negotiations to buy our first and only house. I assisted him in securing a car loan and a mortgage and most of the family financial business. As a child I really was not prepared to take on this role, but necessity made it unavoidable. I remember always feeling the tremendous weight of needing to protect my parents and feeling nervous that I would give them bad advice or lead them into poor decisions that would harm our family.

As our sojourn in the U.S. increased, my family became more rooted in their community and familiar with English and life in America. Over the years my parents had established some strong friendships and relationships. They were very active in their parish and were recognized in the Latino community for their service and leadership. Having become sufficiently secure and established, they had begun to assist others during rough times and periods of transition such as those they had experienced. A major focus of their volunteer efforts was with the resettlement of refugees from Vietnam and from the 1980 Cuban Mariel exodus, and Mexican migrant workers who were locating in Lincoln. As had been done earlier for them, they sponsored several Vietnamese and Cuban families who lived us while they established themselves in their new home.

My parents' courage, compassion, perserverance, and strong sense of social responsibility greatly influenced me. Perhaps the most powerful lessons I have taken from them were ones that I learned through their actions of concern for others. Their example and my growing awareness of social injustice led me to pursue my studies in the field of social work.

My Journey to the Academy

School has always been a source of great contradiction for me. It is simultaneously where I belong and where I do not. I attended Catholic parochial schools from kindergarten to eighth grade and a city-wide consolidated Catholic high school. In both grade school and high school I excelled in academics. I always received top grades and was placed in honors courses. My school years were punctuated with awards, recognitions, and kudos. I even managed to do relatively well on the standardized tests. I didn't participate in any extra-curricular activities, but I did have friendships and was socially accepted by my peers.

I was constantly rewarded and encouraged to achieve academically by my parents and teachers. This aspect of schooling was very affirming. However, other aspects of my school experience worked against my feeling of belonging. Lincoln, Nebraska, had a small Latino population, and throughout my school years I alternated between being the only or one of two or three Latino students in my class. I was always very aware of this. My first memory from school is of my first day in kindergarten. The teacher was calling roll for the first time and paused at Jesus Ramirez's name. Sister Mary appeared shocked that anyone would dare use the name of God for their child and pronounced it as one would in English rather than the very different Spanish pronunciation. Embarrassed, Jesus asked her to call him "Gus" instead. She quickly accepted this name and it has remained with him ever since. I also remember that I was next on the class list and was thankful that my name was Maria, something the teacher would not have difficulty pronouncing.

I also vividly remember the fall morning when I was in the second grade and I was sworn in as an American citizen alongside my parents and sister. When I returned to school for my afternoon classes I was made to tell my story to each class. The school principal escorted me to the kindergarten through sixth grade classrooms as I was made to explain how I came to the United States on a Boat as a refugee and how thankful I was to now be an "American." This was followed by my recitation of the Pledge of Allegiance. I was the civics lesson for the day.

Other references to Latin America or Latinos were sparse throughout my schooling. When they were discussed, it was always from an arrogant, inaccurate first-world perspective. I remember that the religious sisters who taught us would refer to Latin American countries as "backward" and in need of our assistance. Towards this end, every year our class would "adopt" a Latin American child from some unnamed country. The adoption was secured by a donation of change collected from the children. For our pennies we were given assurances the child we adopted would receive food and a Christian education. In school I learned that to be Latin American was to be inferior, impoverished, uneducated, and unsophisticated. At home my parents tried to correct that portrayal by associating pride with my Latin American heritage, with my ability to speak two languages, with my familiarity with multiple cultures.

In high school again the curriculum and classrooms were noticeably void of a Latino presence. The one exception was the Spanish teacher. As in grade school, the history and contemporary experiences of Latinos and other people of color were omitted or distorted in the curriculum.

While some of my school experiences were painful or anxiety-provoking, they were relatively benign compared to the experiences of most of my Latino and African American friends. My English fluency, my light skin, my red hair and freckles, and middle-class cultural capital spared me a lot of the indignities that they experienced.

It was in college that Latino identity moved beyond simple ethnic identity to a political identity. All of the sudden I began to understand my personal history in a larger context. This process began in my sophomore year, when by chance I enrolled in a social welfare policy course with a professor who provided a progressive critique of the development of the American welfare state. I was intrigued by her perspective and found myself asking for more texts to read, lectures to attend, films to view, and classes to take. She introduced me to her peace and justice work in Central America, to her involvement in the sanctuary movement, and her earlier activism in the welfare and civil rights movement. I enrolled in a course on sociology of gender where I was first exposed to feminist writings, some by women of color. I moved on to take courses on race and inequality, on Native American child welfare, on urban sociology, on social movement theory, and continued to deepen my understanding of what it meant to be Cuban, Latina, a woman. I began to see how my experiences were tied to those of other disenfranchised groups, how the resources and wealth of subordinate nations were appropriated by the West, and of the U.S. imposition of oppressive governments in the Caribbean, Latin America, and Africa.

In order to pay for college and support myself, I began to work full-time in my junior year. My work life further served to inform me of issues of ethnic, racial, gender, and economic inequality. My earliest job in my chosen profession, social work, was as the first executive director of a small Latino community-based social service and cultural center. As I mentioned before, Lincoln had a small Latino population, but it also had a small African American and Native American population. Each community had its own center and faced similar issues of poverty, unemployment, discrimination, high rates of incarceration, oppressive work conditions, and unequal educational opportunities. The three centers worked independently as well as collaboratively on many issues and had many challenges and successes. The collaborative work between the agencies and communities introduced me to the importance and force of multiracial solidarities.

I learned many invaluable lessons from the people I worked alongside with at the center. It was because of my experiences there that I decided to continue in social work, but with a focus on community organizing and social welfare policy, rather than social work practice with individuals. However, I felt quite unprepared to do this, so I decided to go to a graduate program with a focus on social welfare policy. I ended up at the University of Chicago's School of Social Service Administration. Again this was a turning point for me.

In Chicago I found myself for the first time surrounded by a large and active Latino and African-American community. I had moved to the city during Mayor Harold Washington's first term. He had nurtured a multiracial coalition that made him the first African-American mayor of the city. It was a tremendously hopeful and active time. Poor communities that had suffered from years of disinvestment were suddenly being given needed dollars, community-based efforts seemed to be making gains, and solidarities were forged between African Americans, Latinos, Asian Americans, and White progressives.

I lived in a predominantly Puerto Rican community and worked to support myself while I continued my studies. During these years I held several jobs: a counselor with displaced steel workers, a case manager for Latino adults with chronic mental illness, a researcher for a child welfare reform organization, and primary investigator on a state-wide needs assessment project for Latinos with developmental disabilities. All of these experiences further informed my understanding of social issues and my commitment to social work with a justice focus.

At the University of Chicago I had the opportunity to study with other Latino and African-American students who had similar perspectives and convictions. This was very rewarding and supportive experience in many ways. Interestingly, we were first drawn together as a group following the comments of a White classmate during a class discussion on affirmative action. He stated that he would be pained by the constant wondering about whether he had gotten a job or into a school like the University of Chicago because of his skin color rather than his academic qualifications. We looked at each other in horror as we saw some nods indicating agreement, some comments in support, and silence on the part of others. While I had not contributed much to the class discussions thus far in the quarter, I could not remain silent this time. I ignored my fears and responded to his comment by indicating that as a middle-class White man he should expect his concerns about preferential treatment to be heightened, given the privilege afforded to people like him. After class all of the students of color remained and so our friendships began, as well as our efforts towards developing a multicultural student organization.

Some of the relationships I developed at school during this time have continued to be of great importance to me. It is now ten years since my graduation from the University of Chicago and I still have personal and professional relationships with several of my classmates who were involved in the development of the student organization. Also, while at the University of Chicago I had two professors who took an interest in me. Both encouraged me to continue in my studies, and for the first time I began to remotely consider doctoral education.

My Experience in the Academy

In some ways it is rather odd that I ended up in academia. I entered into graduate school with no intentions of becoming an academic. I enjoyed the policy research that I was doing for state government, as well as the community work, and wished to stay in the same type of activities. Yet I wanted to enhance my research skills and temporarily break from my work life to accomplish some of the reading and exploring I didn't have time to do otherwise. With these goals in mind I began my doctoral studies. It wasn't until I was writing my dissertation that I began to consider the prospect of teaching.

Now, on the other side of the desk, the university continues to be a place where I am both rewarded and marginalized. I've been rewarded with some very sustaining relationships with several colleagues, outlets for my research and writing, some wonderful students, and opportunities. I am very fortunate that my teaching responsibilities correspond directly with my interests and research. I teach several courses related to social policy, community organizing, and race, ethnicity and gender.

While my life has been made richer in many ways through my relationship to the university, I have also experienced some loneliness and some displacement in the academy. Once again, school has placed me in a context in which I am the only Latina. My years of community practice and Latino-focused state initiatives had surrounded me with other Latino professionals, communities, and projects that were close to my heart. Joining the academy has in some ways removed me from this, but I have been very conscious and deliberate about extending my university work through collaborative research projects and service that connects me to the people, communities, and issues I am committed to and nurtured by. Fortunately, the university has been supportive and given me the space to do so.

Another dimension of my identity that has marked my experience in the academy has been my gender and my caretaking relationships. I am the mother of two young children and I also care for my parents, who live with us. My mother is suffering from Alzheimer's and my father is terminally ill. My son was three years old when I joined the faculty at my institution and in my first year there I became pregnant with my daughter. I am the first tenure-track faculty member to ever have a pregnancy and birth while on faculty at our school. There have been some subtle and not so subtle comments made to me that suggest perceptions some colleagues have about combining family and scholarship. Furthermore, within social work the area of social policy has been dominated by males and my department reflects this, with only one other woman teaching in this area. However, in recent years several women with children have joined our faculty, somewhat normalizing the experience of being a mother and a serious scholar. Furthermore, the women faculty have begun to meet in recent years for the purpose of examining our place in the school and the university and providing support and guidance to each other.

Conclusion

I began this essay with the story of my family and I find myself returning to it in closing. The unexpected events in my family's life have in some way been paralleled in my individual life. They came to the United States, and more specifically Lincoln, Nebraska, quite by accident. Not unlike their voyage to America, my journey into academia was not carefully planned or anticipated. My experiences of the academy has been similar to theirs of the United States as a place that has both marginalized and included them. They have grappled with making this borrowed place their new home. It is a space that they struggled to build and claim, and it is a project that continues, similar to the one I have undertaken in the academy.

Chapter 9

Processing

Aminah B. McCloud

Each of us has the right and the responsibility to assess the roads which lie ahead, and those over which we have traveled, and if the future road looms ominous or uncompromising, and the roads back uninviting, then we need to gather our resolve and, carrying only the necessary baggage, step off that road into another direction. If the new choice is also unpalatable, without embarrassment, we must be ready to change that as well.

Wouldn't Take Nothing for My Journey Now.
Maya Angelou

In this particular recounting I relate my recent experiences as a Muslim African-American female associate professor of Islamic studies. Teaching at a predominately white, private university in one the most segregated cities in the Midwest is definitely a challenge. Fortunately, at my school there are a number of faculty and administrators concerned with the issues surrounding the experiences of faculty of color. Unfortunately this concern does not spread to students. White students in the 1990s in the Midwest, in particular, seem to have missed out on history. Before I recount the story of one class that exemplifies my teaching experience, I need to give readers a short explanation of why this particular story and no other one fulfills the mission of this text and a biography.

When asked to tell a story about an incident that changed by teaching, I jumped at the opportunity. Then when I began to review the outstanding moments I found that my war stories were very different in content and my reactions were not always pedagogical. For instance, some classes forced me to learn to make every set of directions very explicit, leaving no room for the imagination; while others made the focus the need to be firm about absences, late assignments, and so on. The story I realized that forced me to actually reassess my teaching is the story I am going to tell. Let me tell you who I am first.

I graduated from college as a science major, pursued a degree in forensic pathology, and taught science and math for a few years before finishing pharmacy school. After practicing pharmacy for a few years (and being robbed several times), I switched to work full time as a physician's assistant in a private practice. Take a breath, the story does not end here! Finally, I returned to graduate school for a Ph.D. in Islamic studies as a result of religious commitment and the need for African-American Muslims to pursue knowledge, conduct research, and produce scholarship in this area. Needless to say, I enjoyed every tortuous moment of this path and have used everything I have learned along the way to inform my current teaching. Teaching is at the core of what I do in my life. The challenge of sharing with students, listening to them to gain even more knowledge, watching their discoveries, and discovering with them is one of most exhilarating, ongoing experiences in life.

Having gone to college in the sixties, I assumed that the protests over the Vietnam War, the civil rights and black power movements had forever changed the soul of America. This is not because I was fantasizing. Perhaps because I lived in an integrated neighborhood in an east coast city, would send my children to private Quaker schools, enjoyed the friendships of people from around the world, I believed it. Well, the Midwest has certainly sobered my thoughts. I had never heard a white adult use the word "nigger" in my presence until I joined academe. I had never had a group of white adults accuse me of anything until I began university teaching in the Midwest. I have taught years in an orthodox Jewish high school, in Quaker schools, in junior college, and in the university as a graduate instructor and have never seen the peculiar racism I have experienced in this university. But now let me tell this story.

As a professor in an academic area which had no course listings, I had to write several courses and was encouraged and given the freedom to do so. One of those courses is entitled Islam in the United States. Since this is my research specialty, I was delighted to be able to design and teach this course. The first time teaching this course has, however, forever changed me and my teaching. Prior to this experience, I (like other professors of color, I suspect,) had experienced rudeness, challenges to authority, and dismissiveness from students. This experience, however, temporarily took away my sense of myself because of its threatening nature.

After carefully taking students through the "housekeeping" (what this course is about, grading, and so on) portion of the syllabus, we needed to discuss why this course was important, the interdisciplinary nature of the subtopics and most importantly, the highly sensitive nature of the some of the issues we would cover. In this course we had to discuss slavery, racism, civil rights, black nationalism, Islam, influences from the Muslim world and present day rhetoric from Muslim communities. There was wide-ranging diversity in this class: African, African American, Asian, Arab, Pakistani, European, Latino, and Russian—students who were Muslim, Catholic and Protestant Christian, Jewish, and Buddhist. For some reason all of these students wanted to know something about Islam in America.

In my pedagogy, I engage students in conversation, encourage them to be honest in their talk, and try to be honest myself. A part of this engagement is to begin classes with a lecture/discussion on critical thinking, values and assumptions. As we explore our values through discussion of issues, often students find that they continuously make decisions based on values they don't even know they have and are unable to articulate when and where those values emerged. We use the intimacy that comes from these discussions to begin to explore other communities. I often tell students when I am giving my opinion and always permit them to disagree but demand that both of us provide evidence for our positions. Generally, this position has initially made students uncomfortable but has always resulted in a genuine learning atmosphere after the shock.

During the first two classes, during the introduction, I noticed that one student, a Russian Jewish male, challenged almost every statement I made. He did not think that the class should talk about American slavery but if we had to, then we should discuss it as an economic phenomenon without political and social ramifications. He also felt that to accuse the West of racism was "old" and really not an accurate assessment of the basis for the problems of Africans in this country. He stated that to call the enslavement of Africans in this country a "holocaust" was totally incorrect because there was only one holocaust and it would remain the only holocaust. Discussion of religion in America also upset him because he did not think that I was qualified to speak on the subject. He felt that I was "by nature" biased because I was African American, Muslim, and female. While this barrage was certainly unsettling, I did not hesitate to tackle each issue and encourage him to listen and reflect. Leaving class however, the thoughts about the potential for class chaos, wear and tear on my spirit began. It did not occur to me until the next day that the problem was his perception of me.

At home, thinking about how to get a handle on this situation before it got out of hand, I realized that for most of my students I was a "Black Muslim." By this I mean the Black Muslims of C. Eric Lincoln's text, *The Black Muslims of America*—members of Elijah Muhammad's community now led by Louis Farrakhan. Although smiling at this thought, since I am not nor have ever been a member of this community, but thinking of the picture that would paint, I began to see from the student's point of view.

In addition to having an African-American female professor for the first time, my students were confronted with my being Muslim and all of the stereotypes the word conjures up. When introducing myself to students I have always identified myself as Muslim; therefore, I did not consider the problems students might perceive. Islam was however, only one aspect of my dilemma; I needed to reassess what and how I was doing in the classroom. But before any assessment could begin the next class took place.

In this class, the Russian Jewish student was again on the attack. I made several references to the turmoil present in the religious environment in America, during the last two decades of the nineteenth and the first three decades of the twentieth centuries. In the course of giving an overview of a very complex religious history, I made a reference to social Darwinism as an outgrowth of Darwin's theories and how the notion of "the survival of the fittest" became a further scientific justification for racism. My student asserted that he had two courses in biology and one in history which validated his stance that there was no connection and that I had "no right to include science in my lectures" and further that "the authorities should be notified because I was teaching lies in the classroom." The gasps of his peers were audible and I must admit my reaction at this outburst was one of incredulity. The student continued, stating that his history professor had unequivocally stated that there was no link between social Darwinism (which had been misappropriated) and Darwin's theories. My immediate retort was that for the time being I was teaching this class and until I was convinced otherwise, the lecture would stand. At the close of class I strongly suggested that we make an appointment to meet in my office.

Back in my office, I was reeling with anger, embarrassment, and frustration. I talked to several colleagues, relating the incidents, looking for reasons and solutions. Each suggested, independently, that I remove his name from my roll and put an end to an incredible encounter, but only after having a meeting with the student. I also needed to inform my department chairman. My original plan for reassessment was recrafted to include the question how could one so young be so close-minded? What was this student challenging? Was he protesting my femaleness or blackness or was this a Jewish challenge to Islam? Did he perceive me a "Black Muslim" who hated Jews? Was it all of these identities? At his age could he know the background and implications of his protest? Or perhaps he was just an obnoxious, arrogant young man, mad at everyone.

This clearly was not a class where my usual assumptions of what students knew about American or world history, social order, or science held true. This student felt that he not only had the right to challenge the course but he also had an obligation to challenge my being. This wasn't a situation where what I said mattered. This was a situation where one student was turning a class (an elective) into chaos. In a teaching institution, this dilemma handled without careful consideration is potentially either a suicide or homicide for either the professor or the student. In a tuition-driven institution, the student is always right if the professor is a person of color and usually right even if the professor is a satellite link. This was not simply an issue of students proclaiming and adhering to "an Eurocentric, Western point of view" where I could inject notions of other worldviews (Page 1993; 64). While I had developed a pedagogy, or so I thought, around raising the awareness level of students, sharing and learning in familiar environment, I had not given voice to my own critical consciousness in a way that prepared a soldier for war. I had reflected in separate spheres on the images of African-American women, Muslim women, African-American Muslim women, female professors, African-American female professors, and Muslims. Since I inhabit each of these spaces, the conversation took the shape of the space and remarkably the spaces rarely converge. The critical consciousness in each of these spaces is unique—their convergence is probably a level I avoid both consciously and unconsciously. I know that empowerment comes from understanding and acting from a knowledge of one's experiences. The problem resides in even beginning to give voice to that space where the conversations become emulsified, but let me return to my tale.

The student came to my office and with one other professor (from my faculty as insurance) present, I proceeded to lay out for him my view of his actions in crystal-clear terms. I told him that I believed that he had attacked my integrity and that the attack was intentional. Further, due to that attack I felt that there was nothing I or the course could offer him, and his withdrawal, without (financial) penalty, would be greatly appreciated. Lest he miss my point, I demanded that we go to the registrar's office and take care of this business immediately. The young man responded with great alarm and protest that he was neither racist nor sexist and certainly had nothing against me as a Muslim. My colleague (a white female) asserted that since he did not dispute the facts of the encounters that his behavior belied his current assertions. She inquired as to why he would want to remain in a class that was so poorly taught by a racist who gave bogus information. His answer was that he was "just challenging." He had solicited corroboration from his white history professor who affirmed that he was correct in both his statements and behavior.

Both of us asked if this was his normal behavior in the classroom; to this he answered negatively. I, in earnest, repeated my suggestion that he withdraw from the course because I would not tolerate challenges to either my integrity or class authority; I could not permit him to put the class in chaos; and finally, I could not grade fairly due to his hostility and my anger. This student continued to protest my suggestion and pleaded to be given a chance to understand what I was trying to accomplish with the class. I suggested that we postpone any decision until I consulted further with my colleagues and department chair again. I promised to contact him within five days with a final resolution to the problem.

The very next day (not a class day) the entire class came to my office to offer their assessment of the student and the class. Many of these students knew him from other classes and contexts. They informed me that he was a leading member of one of the student Jewish organizations and had written several anti-Arab, anti-Muslim articles which they had copied for me. All of the students declared him racist, most felt there was sexism involved, and many were confused by his anti-Muslim stance and his rationale for taking the course. Listening to their issues/concerns, I asked them to reflect on those concerns of theirs about which they felt passionately and then give voice to how they address those issues in various contexts. What if he was doing the same, albeit rudely with hostility? I did not expect immediate reflection from them and suggested that we could spend a part of the next class exploring the issues.

Further consultation with my department chair and other faculty members elicited myriad suggestions, all centering on the need to "get him out of the class." Why this was the only solution seemed to be the result of a show of force by faculty over the obvious implications of the student's behavior and insinuations. How to restore my integrity and that of the class was a far more difficult question. While the direct removal of the student from the classroom seemed the best resolution, it did not "feel right." Should I, in the face of bullying, insult, and hostility, exert the ultimate authority, or should I put an additional burden on my back and try to move this student from one space to another? I decided that I am not a "we shall overcome" believer nor does my pedagogy, real or imagined, lend itself to resorts to ultimate power (except in my house).

Can you imagine the personal turmoil when one's assertion of presence in the public space is on recall? What went wrong with a thoughtful and critical pedagogy? Well, I cannot state that I was or am capable of a full analysis of this dilemma but I did find out some very useful things. First, even though I thought that I had read and done a lot of reflection on teaching the "other" from my perspective, I had only looked at issues revolving around teaching students of the majority American culture that their way of seeing the world was only one way of gazing.

The prevailing texts and conversations on multiculturalism direct us to uncovering information hidden by the powerful in their articulations of knowledge in the world. Opening students' minds to the way the world is perceived by minorities, oppressed peoples, and other majority cultures was where I located my task. They needed to expand their vision and knowledge about what was all around them. I needed to provide a classroom that afforded nurturing and safety. I needed to liberate them from narrowness and to liberate myself by constantly seeking ways to tell the story. I had to be honest about who I was, and thus inspire them to honesty and reflection. What I had not learned or rather did not critique was the "who I was," and why the notion to liberate.

As a result of my own internalization of oppression in America, my view is also quite narrow. I assume that when students come into contact with me there is one prevailing set of stereotypes—those about African-Americans. But even this knowledge is not an accurate reflection on what is really in their minds nor mine. I am on guard, waiting to be trivialized and marginalized, because experience has taught me that it is inevitably going to arrive. I must prove that in spite of my blackness, I am educated and can share knowledge. On the other side of the equation is the fact that I have stereotyped them and the notion of liberating them can be problematic. The position in which one has to place oneself in order to conceptualize a liberation is increasingly more difficult for me to accept.

As an African American constantly engaged in resisting racism I see the world as an outsider for whom there is no utopia. I am battle-ready every day, and the awareness level I must maintain is beyond what the current self-help texts seek to explore. I need very badly for my white students to understand who I am and for my black students to have some affirmation of their being. But this identity is rooted in my Muslimness and femaleness. For these identities I have not prepared myself for battle, and it is obvious in my pedagogy. In gearing up for a white audience I have always thought my being a black professor the major issue. The question of how to teach from a position of a triply stereotyped other had never occurred to me in ways that shaped my pedagogy. Neither had the critical question of why liberation as opposed to some other kind of goal. Had I bought such notions into my teaching, although giving it my own twist, without real reflection? These were new avenues to travel.

When I asked myself what had been my experience of learning, the answer, or at least part of the answer, was: I expanded my knowing, which gave me a wider field from which to assess things around me for decision-making and action. To know did not liberate me from anything in particular as much as it enhanced self-awareness, self-esteem, and proactive activity. Knowing did not give me a "saving" attitude nor did it change my particular circumstance, but it did give me information with which to be able to change the points of view on my circumstances.

Upon careful consideration, I decided to let this student stay in class, not take any additional burdens on myself of "liberating" him, and focus on letting all of my personal and social identities speak. I decided that to know about the subject of any course I teach is important, not just as another way of seeing but because to not know about something so important is to be uneducated. My courses inform and give information on the world and engage students in serious reflection about what I teach and who all of us are who are exploring. To gain knowledge is one objective of an university education. My attempts to provide a nurturing and safe environment to gain that knowledge still go on with even more attention to the politics of social identity.

Back in the classroom, I began the next class with a ten-minute talk on the issues of the what, whose, and the why of what we call knowledge. The emphasis was on the synthesis of experience and fact. Rather than give students a fact without some knowledge of how that fact came to be, I spelled out the influencing factors or gave them suggested readings. Rather than assume they needed to be liberated from something and that I was in any respect that liberator, I chose to treat the classroom as a laboratory—though not a sterile one. We continued to be honest about who we are as the researchers—as honest as folks can be in a classroom but not so much so that the personal gets in the way of our task. This is a delicate balance.

The student in question stayed in the class but did not continue to attack me nor disrupt the class. I don't think this class changed many of his feelings but it did change how he had to handle himself in relation to others. As for me, I am in process. At least one aspect of the process seems to be challenging the prevalent notions of the teacher as liberator. I cannot say where I am going with this challenge, but I have discovered that my students are helpful guides who have sometimes a startling patience with my plight and an active willingness to assist me on my way, occasionally joining me on the journey. I am assessing the balance that must be maintained between honesty and information and reassessing my own stake in power and authority.

Reference List

Angelou, Maya. 1993. *Wouldn't Take Nothing for My Journey Now*. New York: Random House. p. 24.

Page, Helán E. 1993. *"Teaching Comparative Social Order and Caribbean Social Change,"* in *Spirit, Space and Survival*. Eds. Joy James and Ruth Farmer. New York: Routledge, p. 64.

Chapter 10

"Have YOU Ever Lived on Brewster Place?": Teaching African-American Literature in a Predominantly White Institution

Clare Oberon Garcia

During a course on black women's literature I was teaching a couple of years ago, we were studying Ann Petry's naturalistic study of an ambitious single mother's life in the inner city, *The Street*. After class, as I chatted with some students who had lingered to ask questions, I mentioned—I don't remember in connection with what—that I had been to school in Switzerland. One young woman expressed astonishment, and then proceeded to tell me what she had seen as my life's story: "I pictured you working your way through high school and college, in somewhere like Chicago, struggling through with all your children, and then finally getting this job at our college." Laughing, I explained to her that I had had a rather middle-class childhood, gone to private schools, had my children *after* I married an attorney, and had been living in Colorado for five years before I joined the college faculty. I wondered how many other students had seen me as their local version of Petry's Lutie Johnson, or as one of the women of Brewster Place, or the up-close-and-personal illustration of a *Time* magazine story on successful workfare.

I teach several African-American and American literature classes at a small, predominantly white liberal arts college. I have never had more than two black students in a single class, and at most I have had four students of color in one class. Certain things happen in my African-American literature classes which simply don't happen in my

American literature classes, although writers of color are included in all of the classes I teach. In conversations with other minority faculty at predominantly white institutions, I've discovered that these issues aren't unique to my experience. In fact, an hour ago I had lunch with a young black man who was interviewing for a position on our faculty. We asked him how his classes responded to his teaching strategies, which were very "real world" oriented. "The vast majority of kids in my class are white," he said. "And they sit there looking at me as if I were from Public Enemy."

The new emphasis on multiculturalism in education and the revisions of the canons of several disciplines have meant that many white undergraduates are being exposed to the creative and scholarly work of minorities. In addition, thanks to increased recruitment efforts, more and more minority faculty are teaching in predominantly white institutions. I've found that the issues of authority, anxiety, and what I call "emotional baggage" come up again and again. To be an effective teacher, I must address them.

On the first day of class, I encourage students to talk about their interest in taking the class. Many white students express the fear that they won't understand the texts because they come from such different worlds. Several times, especially in my black women's fiction classes, I've had students preface remarks with, "As a white, middle-class male . . ." Sometimes the qualifier is merely an excuse for not engaging in the discussion or the reading. But more often it reveals the speaker's anxiety that he or she isn't "getting" something which is apparent to readers who have either race or gender in common with the author of the book. I try to convey to the students that there are no privileged readings in my class—only readings which are more or less interesting than others.

I also try to establish a classroom climate where students can actively question their own biases as well as those of the author and other readers. I encourage students to feel that they can speak freely without being self-conscious about their lack of knowledge, experience, or political savvy. Merely telling them they are free in this way is not enough, of course, so I try to model different responses to the texts for them. I do this in several ways. I might take lines of interpretation which aren't "politically correct." Or I share the processes of my own reading and rereading. For example, when teaching Ralph Ellison's *Invisible Man*, I compare my initial rather confused readings of the book with later readings, when I was familiar with most of the allusions. I emphasize that we are *all* readers, and if our readings are more interesting than others' it isn't necessarily because of "what we have in common" with the author or the protagonist. And of course, the texts themselves challenge any preconceptions the students may have about any kind of monolithic "black experience in the United States." If anything, all my students come away with a sense of the rich variety of black experience in literature, black aesthetics, and black ideologies.

As in all English classes, the question of which readings are superior to others raises the issue of authority. Yet again, the racial dimension adds an extra twist or two to an already complex problem. When I taught Black Literature in America last year, at least half of the twenty-five students in the class came to me individually to express consternation that there weren't any minority students in the class. So I decided that we needed to talk about these feelings *as* a class. I asked: What was it that they expected any minority student, as a minority, to contribute to the class? We had been reading texts from slave narratives to sketches of black bourgeois angst, from the uncompromising anger of Richard Wright to the genteel humanism of Charles Johnson. Yet the consensus of the class was that any black student, no matter what his or her background, would be able to "help the white students understand the books better," because the black student would have "actually lived" the situations depicted in the various texts.

The conversation led to the issue of my authority as the only black person in the room, and whether or not they would take this course if it were taught by a white teacher. The vast majority of the class said that they wouldn't, even though most teachers on our English faculty include texts by writers of color in their courses. I then asked the class if they felt that I shouldn't teach Henry James (my dissertation subject) and other white writers. Perhaps out of politeness, they agreed that *this* was all right, as black people "have always had to learn the ways of the dominant culture," and I had a Ph.D. from a "white" university. I concluded, privately, that the issue of authority is a double-edged sword. I would always be expected to have an extra insight into black texts—especially black women's texts—just by virtue of experience. And perhaps on some level this is true. But I also realized that they don't see black literature, or black scholarship, as on a par with traditional literary scholarship or the Euro-American canon. A working-class Jewish woman from Brooklyn can become a expert on Shakespeare or Baudelaire, in their view, if she masters the language, the texts, and the critical literature. But they would not grant that a middle-class white man could ever be a trusted authority on Toni Morrison.

Because we live in such a racially polarized society, students bring a lot of "emotional baggage" with them to a black literature class. Their experiences with black boyfriends, black maids, their perceptions of cliquish black students in their own high schools, their impressions of black life that they glean from television, MTV, or—in one case—a tourist's drive-by of Cabrini-Green, the infamous Chicago housing project, all influence their perception of what the course is about and texts that they read. My challenge as a teacher is to discern which baggage it is educational for the whole class to unpack and analyze, and which baggage must be dealt with in other areas of the students' life. I used to set aside a session early in the class which I called, to myself, "a rap session." Here I let the students "let it all hang out" in a freewheeling conversation in which they confronted and shared their own doubts, prejudices, fears, questions, and notions about race. I thought that these rap sessions would allow us to clear the air and then get down to the business of reading texts. However, I found that emotions came up in these classes which I was unprepared to handle: a biracial student exploding in anger about high-school incidents which still smarted, a white student expressing wonder at how much he didn't know about the life of the black maid who had served his family for over twenty years, the descendant of Virginian slave owners weeping in guilt. . . . I haven't entirely abandoned the idea of allowing the students to examine how their own experiences influence their reading, but I now insist that class discussions be focused, structured, and rooted in the particular issues raised by the texts. I have the students do a lot of small group work in which I don't participate directly, and I suspect that a lot of these issues are dealt with in conversations outside of class with each other.

Finally, I encourage the students to take risks. I am always impressed by how brave most of the students who take my classes are. Many of them have read works by black authors before my class—either in other classes or, more often, on their own. They are excited by the new territory of African-American literature. They are open to new perspectives on history, social structures, relationships, and their own privileges.

Teaching in a predominantly white college where there is only one other African-American woman on the faculty can be bewildering and lonely, but it is my students' enthusiasm and patience that sustain me. I always try to meet them wherever they are, and guide them to places they might not have imagined.

Chapter 11

Native(s) in the Classroom: Displacement and Cultural Politics

Fassil Demissie

All classrooms topographies are unreadable without a specific legend. I offer my legend at the beginning. This essay charts the geography of classrooms at DePaul University where I have been teaching for the last seven years as an assistant professor in urban studies. By looking at the classroom as a site of dominant relations and master narratives, I hope to develop an account of the politics of teaching. Classrooms are not just physical spaces deeply inscribed with all sorts of contradictions; they are also spaces where the politics of identity, teaching, and learning are negotiated.

From There to Here

A remarkable phenomenon of the twentieth century has been the massive movement of peoples and cultures through physical displacement, as refugees, immigrants, migrants, exiles, or expatriates. This staggering and disorienting displacement of peoples and cultures across the globe has not yet run its course. Yet, states and governments have responded to this social, political, and economic phenomenon by erecting administrative, legal, and physical barriers to stem the displacement of people across national and international boundaries.

Unlike the nineteenth century, when colonial and imperial enterprises fueled large transcontinental settlements of Europeans which displaced the indigenous peoples, contemporary displacements from the periphery to the center have set in motion xenophobia and racism in all spheres of public and private life. As subjects displaced from the periphery to the center, the presence of natives in the classroom is leading to the articulation of new contradictions about new cultural politics, identity, and forms of representation. It is these issues I want to explore through my own autobiography.

I was born in Addis Ababa, Ethiopia, at a particular moment in the history of the country. I attended the Balabat School not far from my family's home. I grew up with a distinct interest in pursuing education overseas which was carefully nourished and sustained by a large number of British, American, and Indian instructors who taught at Balabat. Attending Balabat School was particularly interesting, partly because over the years before my entry, the school had begun to accept students from other socioeconomic backgrounds, and as result, I had the opportunity to develop friendships in a limited way with some of my fellow classmates whose social backgrounds were very different from my own. My limited interaction with them outside my narrow circle of friends introduced me to the deep class divisions within the society where I grew up and made me conscious of my own privileged position in it. I was constantly reminded about the class divisions when I walked home from school. Unlike other cities where class segregation assumes a particular spatial dimension, the neighborhood where I grew up manifested class difference in a particular way. Here rich and poor families lived in close proximity and the markers of class identity were embodied in the particular houses families occupied in the neighborhood. As I walked home from school, I saw daily the material inscription of poverty and destitution. Although people would say hello to me as I passed by their crumbling one-room houses, I always noticed the way people looked at me. It was a look of palpable hostility. As a teenager, it was hard for me to figure out why people in the neighborhood looked at me in a particular way. At that time, I did not understand their resentment and rancor towards me and other members of my family.

The last year of high school was particularly interesting as I was making plans to continue my college education in the United States. I had written to a number of colleges in California, Wisconsin, Missouri, Texas, and Tennessee on the advice of a number of American Peace Corps teachers who taught at my school. My own sense of "America," its people and educational system was a product of information and advice I had received from people I knew, as well as friends of mine who had gone to the U.S. to study. The books and glossy magazines I had been reading about "America" shaped my own superficial understanding about it. In addition, the United States Information Agency (USIA) in the center of town provided a highly distorted narrative and powerful images which obscured in fundamental ways the history and contemporary realities of the country and its people, particularly regarding issues of ethnicity and race.

When I first arrived in the U.S. to attend the University of California, at Berkeley, I faced a number of critical questions about my own identity. Growing up in a society where people were not categorized by "race," I had many problems completing university forms that required individuals to identify themselves by "race." Finding the "racial" categories in the application forms—"White," "Black," "Hispanic," "Pacific Islander," and "Asian"—unhelpful, I consistently marked the box for "Other" and wrote, "from earth." What appeared initially to be a maze of forms quickly revealed a matrix of racialized underpinnings of ideas about "race" and "racial" classifications. The "racial" classifications embedded in the forms were part of a wider discourse about "race," its language and thesis. This particular form of "racial" categorization was outside my consciousness, and I had had no idea about my own "racial" identity when I grew in Ethiopia. For the first time, I became keenly aware of "racial" markings in American society and my own ambivalence towards them. I had no awareness of the "racial" classification or consciousness that W. E. B. DuBois so cogently wrote about. For me, it became the beginning of a slow and painful process of constructing a "racial" self, of becoming "Black," learning and acting "Black." There was nothing in my culture to rely upon as a resource to make sense of "racial" identity or to interrogate the "racialized" notions of identity deeply embedded in American society. There are no words in the language I spoke (Amharic) for "race," and hence I had no understanding of what "race" was as it had been constructed in America.

Coming from a society which had no colonial history, and thus no pernicious baggage that has shaped the lives of millions of people in America, I was able to negotiate "racial" identity in a different terrain, which gave me room to maneuver without accepting the terms of "racial" classifications of American society or the alleged "inferiority" complex of being "Black." It was the cultural resource of growing up in a society without the burden of "racial" classification or consciousness that enabled me to negotiate my own identity as "Ethiopian" and "Black" in the context of encounters with western racism.

Initially, most people I have met in school and elsewhere were quite aware, at least superficially, of "Ethiopia" as "Land of Queen Sheba and King Solomon." Occasionally, the then "Emperor Haile Selassie" was added to give some sense about the history of the country. While "Ethiopian" culture, music, and cuisine have become consumable commodities in major metropolitan cities like Washington, D.C., New York, Los Angeles, Atlanta, Chicago, and San Francisco, there is little if any understanding of Ethiopia, its culture, history, and politics. I believe it is the absence of these critical understandings that makes the country's history and people shrouded in mystery and exoticism.

My first few months in this country were marked by constant comments from people I had come across about how "Ethiopians" were very "beautiful" and "charming," how their "distinctive physically features" made them very "different" from the rest of Africans, etc. In addition, there were the usual comments about how fluently I spoke English and how my accent was "attractive."

Whatever notions I had about myself as an "Ethiopian," I also had to come to terms with being an immigrant—a status rife with racialized meanings and images. During the first few years of college, I had to come to terms with being placed in another category, that of "resident alien." I clearly remember sitting across the desk at the Immigration and Naturalization Service (INS) from a middle-aged white woman who was processing my "resident alien" papers. I provided her with all the required documents and information: current photographs, health certificates, fingerprints, family history, and my own personal experiences for the past ten years. The INS agent also inquired whether "I was or ever have been a member a Communist Party or have ever advocated or plotted to overthrow the government of the United States." Having been satisfied with my responses, her anxieties were very visible in the tenor of her voice as she told me that the processing of my papers would take some time before I become a "resident alien." Later, having been conferred the status of "resident alien," I moved to Chicago to teach at DePaul University, some four miles north of downtown Chicago in a predominantly gentrified neighborhood.

Local Knowledge and the Classroom

DePaul University is a located in Lincoln Park—a neighborhood which extends westward from Lake Michigan between Armitage Avenue on the south, to Diversey Parkway on the north. Over the past decade or so, the boundaries of Lincoln Park have been a subject of considerable debate among a dozen civic groups and neighborhood associations.

The original settlement of Lincoln Park dates back to the 1860s, when the McCormick Theological Seminary established a campus on land donated by two wealthy landowners, Joseph Sheffield and William Ogden. Much of the funds for building the seminary came from industrialist Cyrus Hall McCormick. Not far from the McCormick Theological Seminary, the St. Vincent DePaul parish was established in 1875. Although the university was not established until 1898, the area soon became a preferred residential area. Throughout the first three decades of the twentieth century, Lincoln Park continued as an upper class residential district close to the downtown commercial areas as well as the lakefront. Despite the fact that the area attracted a considerable number of affluent families, Lincoln Park also had a significant working-class, Spanish-speaking population. In addition, African-American neighborhoods were squeezed between factories or in close proximity to a corridor of light industry along the Chicago River. The Second World War had a considerable impact on the housing stock in Lincoln Park, as many of the units were subdivided or converted into rooming houses. As more and more families began to move from Lincoln Park to the suburbs during the immediate years of the post-war period, many sections of Lincoln Park declined rapidly. It was not until the late 1960s and early 1970s that concerted revitalization began to affect the character of the neighborhood.

Gentrification speeded up the transformation of Lincoln Park, and as a result, many working-class families were forced out of the area by skyrocketing housing prices and escalating rents, which made the area very expensive to live in. When I arrived in summer of 1989, Lincoln Park had become a yuppie kingdom and a cultural signifier of material consumption. Like other gentrified neighborhoods throughout America, Lincoln Park is both a place and an "imagined community" that insists on the meaning of particular signs and creates its own fabricated history from the ruins of the past. Where once thriving working-class communities prospered, the gentrification of Lincoln Park has altered the texture and density of the neighborhood. It is amazing how churches, schools, and factories that once gave people a sense of place and identity have since been converted into expensive lofts and condominiums. As one walks through the "imagined community" of Lincoln Park, the recreated row houses, multifamily dwellings, and fake Victorian houses seem more like "theme villages" right out of Walt Disney. This neighborhood provides fertile ground for my teaching about cities and neighborhoods.

In one of the courses I teach on urban restructuring, for example, I take students through the gentrified neighborhood and we examine how the displacement of neighborhoods is structurally related to the rhythms and periodicity of the national and international economy. While gentrification is a particular restructuring of inner-city residential areas, the issues of race, class, gender, and ethnicity are deeply woven into it. Some of my students respond approvingly with enthusiasm to the gentrified Lincoln Park, its manicured lawns, gated houses and fabricated architecture. They note how gentrification has been a positive factor in removing the "bums" and "criminals," "drug dealers and "welfare cheaters" from the neighborhood. Their comments vividly reflect what other people who live in the neighborhood have conveyed to me: that the neighborhood has improved and is such a nice place to live in now. Clearly, Lincoln Park has become more racially and economically homogeneous—a result of a campaign of forced removal of all working-class Latino and African-American families from the area.

Teaching in a university situated within this context provides the substance for examining the intersections of race, class, and gender. The classroom is a particular site and a space in which all sorts of anxieties, fears, and hopes of students are worked out in multiple ways. A majority of students who have taken my courses have had no previous encounter with a Black teacher, let alone a professor, before they came to DePaul. Over the past decade, the pool of students who attend DePaul has come from the suburbs as well as from other smaller towns. Hence, they arrive in the classroom with layers of stereotypes about race, class, gender, and ethnicity. It is often in the classroom where some of these stereotypes are contested and worked out.

Three years ago, I developed a course specifically designed for students who major in international studies as an outgrowth of a course I offered on development and decolonization in Africa. Initially, my intention was to engage the students in considering how ideas about development in Africa, or for that matter in Asia and Latin America, did not arise in a social, institutional, or literary vacuum. Ideas about development were assembled within a vast hierarchical apparatus of knowledge production and consumption sometimes known as the "development industry." A contextual reading of the literature of development in my view therefore has a great deal to say about the apparatus of power and domination within which those texts emerge, circulate, and are then consumed. Despite my intention to offer a course that tackled a postcolonial critique of development, its language, rhetoric, and meaning within different political and institutional contexts, the course was only able to enroll the minimum number of students, and consequently it was not offered again. Hence I decided to offer another course that dealt with some of the broader issues that were central to the course on development and decolonization in Africa. Unlike the previous course title, the new course was titled simply "Global Connections." Surprisingly, the number of students enrolled in this course increased dramatically. I was not sure whether this was because of changes in the title or because of some other factors. At any rate, the new course offered enabled me to expand my original ideas and focus on the broad historical processes which formed the basis for the emergence of a particular relationship between Western societies and those of Africa since the early nineteenth century. The course was also concerned with the processes by which Africa played a critical role in the formation of Western societies and how the societies of Africa came to be represented in various disciplines, including anthropology, literature, the arts, and film. In addition, the course also explored the formation of the discourse which produced "self" and "Others" and closely examined the particular form of knowledge and power which produced the identity of the historical "Other," by drawing examples from a variety of historical and theoretical materials to provide a critical reading of the relationships between Western societies and those of Africa.

In the course we also explored a wide range of writings on colonialism and culture, each broadly defined, and considered the multiple dimensions of the encounters and relationships between colonialism, imperialism, and culture, shifting focuses from the metropolitan center to imperial and postcolonial Africa, attempting to join the two ends of this spectrum together to understand them in their dynamic connection rather than as discrete or neatly bounded domains of history and social interaction.

The ethnic composition of the students enrolled in the course was very limited. Apart from a few students from Malaysia, Japan, Tanzania, and the Dominican Republic, they came from middle-class suburbia with little or no contact with Africans or African-Americans. Initially, students were very uncomfortable discussing how the images of "Africa" and concept of "race" were invented in imperial writings and in popular imagination. As we examined in detail how images of "Africa" and "Africans" came to be represented, many of the students saw the contradiction in the way their knowledge of Africa was constituted. Many of them vividly described and shared negative stories they had heard about Africa and Africans in their schools and in their family settings and how they took the stereotyped images for granted.

Of particular significance in our discussions and reflections was the multiplicity of stereotyped images of Africa and Africans in different historical contexts and configurations, their underlying structures, and how these images came to be constituted, as well as their social and political consequences. We also tackled the relationship between images and power and how relations of dominance are constructed and reproduced in popular culture, as well as how these stereotyped images are normalized and routinized in words and images. In discussing the stereotyped images of Africa and Africans, students acknowledged that the dominant image of how Africa was portrayed was one of primitivism, which expressed itself in Africans being "close to nature," emotional, sexually uninhibited, musical, and so forth. It was painful to hear these negative comments, and to experience the casualness with which students conveyed their remarks, indicative of how their whiteness has given them stereotypes about others, Africans in particular.

During discussions, I also related to them my own idealized images of, for example, African-Americans, which had been influenced primarily by Hollywood films, cartoons, and books, and how these images functioned as a marker of social boundaries and devices of historical distortion. Just as the images and films and books the students have seen about Africa were based on caricatures and stereotypes, my own views of African-American history, the legacy of slavery, and racism were equally distorted. While growing up, I do not ever remember seeing any film or reading any book that provided any account of slavery, colonialism, and racism that have shaped and continue to shape the lives of millions of people. All of the films I saw depicted African-Americans as servants and entertainers as well as Sambo, Coon, Rastus, Tom, Uncle, and Mammy—with tragic consequences.

Images and power interact on a national and global scale and the practice of representing Africa with negative images that started in the nineteenth century still prevail. In the classroom, one is confronted with not only the negative representations of Africa of the past, but—more insidious—contemporary images that circulate instantaneously on TV, computer terminals, and books at a speed far greater than before also reproduce perverse images. For all the wealth of information provided by the electronic revolution, we live in a world largely peopled by characters cut from cardboard images.

What I try to do in my teaching is to get students to critically interrogate these images, reflect upon their own notions about ethnicity, self, Other, and to consider how these images are embedded with assumptions, beliefs, and values which are rooted in power and difference. As constructions of human subjectivity, these images of Others, particularly Natives, populate the imaginations of students and shape how they view them in relationship to others. All these images, I seek to engage them in naming, understanding, challenging, and changing.

Chapter 12

Ni Eres Ni Te Pareces: Academia as Rapture and Alienation

Alicia Chavira-Prado

Standing in a phone booth at UCLA, I was calling home to check on my children and to find out if *the letter* had arrived. The man who was my husband back then said "Yes, it's here. You want me to open it?" My heart pounded, my knees got shaky and weak, and I felt a rock in my stomach but "yes," I said, "go ahead." It was informing me that I had been accepted into the graduate program in the anthropology department. I was stunned and elated. And filled with terror. That terror has become part of my existence, and also part of my resistance in academic life. Years later, when I read bell hooks's (1992) own account of terror I understood it instantly as subjectified difference, exclusion, and disempowerment. As a student, terror silenced me in the classroom. Textbooks, professors, and other students spoke a language foreign to me, even more foreign than English. Their words claimed a power over me because I could not interpret, understand, communicate, or analyze their logic. It was an academic language, a complex of coded intellectualism, of privilege. Even now as a professor, my background clashes with those of colleagues and students I encounter, the vast majority of whom are white and come from backgrounds not entirely alien to the university culture. So the terror waxes and wanes but never really leaves me. It fills me every first day of classes, when students look at the opening classroom door expecting their instructor to enter. When they see me, they look away, dismissing this small-framed brown woman until, instead of taking a seat among them, I proceed to the front of the room and introduce myself and the course. Looks of surprise, even disbelief, transform their faces. Students of color have similar reactions. They all seem to me to have a suspicious curiosity of the mysterious. I, the mysterious Other. It becomes incumbent upon me to legitimize the position I assume at the front of the room. This is probably true for any instructor. What is different for professors of minority status is how perceptions of class, ethnicity, and gender uniquely shape our professional relationships throughout the trajectory of our academic life. The terror yields to sadness when Latino students also perceive me with distance, curiosity, and distrust. This informs me that I have become separated from *mi gente*. I crave the comfort of an unquestioned sense of belonging. *Si, soy Mexicana, Latina, Chicana, mujer, hija, madre, esposa, amiga, pero tambien soy maestra en un mundo muy distinto al cual en que nací y en el que me formé como ser humano. Así que ahora resulta que no soy lo que era ni lo que fuî pero tampoco lo que paresco.*[1]

Academia in the United States is an ambiguous world. On the one hand it represents liberation (hooks 1994) for the historically oppressed because its cornerstone, education, equips us to question critically, thereby enabling our decolonizing process. But academia also is a power player in the politics of domination. It ensnarls us into another form of colonization as it attempts to impose its own language, norms, expectations, and proscriptions, all of which form an academic culture that enshrouds theory and method. As students we are introduced to selected, interpreted phenomena that serve to mold us as professional academicians ultimately shaping how (and how much) we analyze, reason, respond, or contribute to new academic production. An inherent irony, and evidencing our recolonization within academia, is the commonly held notion that much of our intellectual endeavor represents independence, liberation, and empowerment.

The counter-theories represented in the works of feminists, people of color, third-world activists, and gay and lesbian authors fuel our optimism for a transformed academy. They help objectify our subjective resistance, validating difference while denouncing inequality in academia and society. In other words, they signify vindication in our decolonizing process. However, the liberation and empowerment gained by these works of resistance have not been unqualified. As counter-theories they are subjectively ignited and, as such, their effect is temporally vulnerable and spatially bound. Temporally vulnerable because, having flared in recent decades as part of social movements and reforms such as affirmative action, their general effects are largely tied to the fate of these movements and reforms, and spatially bound because their greatest impact has been on our native communities, by raising our political consciousness, reaffirming the value of difference, and rekindling our ethnic pride.

Mainstream academia has limited the production of counter-theories and their subversive and transformative potential. In spite of policy reforms such as affirmative action, institutions and departments continue to employ practices that restrict and discourage equitable involvement of minority group members, thus dominating the politics of representation (a term I borrow from West 1993). As a consequence, epistemology remains impervious to institutionalized reform, promoting an ideological system of biases and power imbalances. For nontraditional academics, feeling demoralized and alienated is a common effect that reduces our chances for survival within the academy.

A prime example of mainstream academia's epistemological stronghold is how departments and nonminority colleagues view our work when it refers to our own communities. Academia's colonizing power is potentially destabilized by the critical reanalysis involved in self-representation. Use of our own material reality as substance for critical inquiry humanizes us and our communities. This can demystify imperialist paradigms that, as in the field of anthropology, have exoticized and thus marginalized our native communities by viewing them as loci of field praxis. Hence, self-representational work is discouraged or prohibited through discrediting labels or attitudes that view it as indicative of a lack of academic rigor or commitment. All of this has contributed to a relatively short history of self-representation, a small constituency, and a political weakness that prevent us from (re)modeling an academy that truly acknowledges, legitimizes, and empowers us against the status quo.

My first taste of academia seduced me. While growing up I prayed to be saved from the same life of factory work that had worn and nearly deafened my young mother. By the time I was eighteen I realized that my baby boy represented the best reason to find a better life. And I had found a real attraction to academia. My husband had been recruited to UCLA after high school with a scholarship and student loans made available through the Upward Bound program. After his first year at UCLA, I was pregnant, and the impending burden of family obligations, combined with a lack of mentorship, resulted in his leaving school. Nevertheless, that year was pivotal for both of us as we were introduced to a culture of privilege. Before we were married I would visit him periodically at the university. The affluence surrounding

UCLA, displayed by more white people than I had ever seen at any one time, made me feel like a tourist on a distant journey. The twenty miles that separated Westwood from east Los Angeles could be measured in social distance. I felt awkward and self-conscious, resentful and envious, yet fascinated by everything I witnessed there. I eavesdropped on intellectual discussions about topics that intrigued me and on a couple of occasions, when my boyfriend invited me to attend his classes, I watched and listened to professors give lectures, and to students take notes and ask intelligent questions, in elegant and architecturally imposing classrooms, and wished that I was one of those students. Although unable to articulate it then, I learned intuitively that academia imparted knowledge selectively, and that accessing that knowledge was the key to power.

Almost eight years, many evening classes, and several community colleges later, I entered UCLA as a transfer student in my junior year. It was here that my decision to pursue anthropology was solidified. After learning that its philosophy embraces cultural diversity and relativism, and of its traditional concern with other cultural communities I felt assured that I had found the niche for my academic career and a way to employ the native insight that my class and ethnicity afforded me. When I entered UCLA I had not yet understood how academic life distances us from our familial and cultural roots. I merely saw it as an achievement that would free me from the bonds of material and intellectual poverty.

My terror was born at UCLA. Through my earlier exposure to the institution I knew that I would have to pay a personal price for being a student there. The cost included a silence I was to observe, guaranteed by the threat of humiliation that I would surely suffer if I publicly exposed in the classroom the disadvantages of my background. The school rewarded my conformity with a flood of new ideas and information that were packaged in academic rhetoric and, as such, left me with many unanswered questions. Late at night, after coming home from work and putting my child to bed, I would search for the answers in books, often unsuccessfully, even though I was always armed with a dictionary (as I continue to need now). Not as hard to understand were lectures and readings about Mexicans and Latinos. I witnessed how the richness of my Mexican culture was subjugated in ethnographic texts produced by people like Oscar Lewis. Their analytical elaborations misconstrued and disparaged endogenous meanings and values or portrayed cultural actors as caricatures devoid of human agency and depth. For the first time, I became aware of a language of domination that (re)presented my culture to me, subordinating it through sterile analyses that reduced it to a mere compilation of nonsensical, even obscene, characteristics. At a visceral level I rejected these imaginary interpretations of my cultural reality. But terror prevented me from articulating my objections in classroom discussions. I also was dissuaded by the assurance of a liberal front within academia. Lewis's work had sparked a controversy on the "culture of poverty" theory, to which years later my professors and books still alluded as proof of academia's liberalism. In reality, of course, the controversy had little effect on remodeling subsequent ethnographic production, as was shown in the absence of writings and discussions that would invite, include, or legitimize the native voice. Hence, I painfully suppressed the desire to speak about my culture in classroom discussions. Only in my mind did I share my native understanding with professors and other students by discussing, for example, the real cultural meaning of fresh-made tamales (social cooperation, family and community ties, the celebration of religious and cultural ritual, the cultural survival of colonial conquest, ecological adaptation, the transcendence of gender barriers, intergenerational bonds, the value of children as cultural renewal and the continuity of life, the socially sanctioned promise of a life-long partnership, and a wealth of other meanings that made tamales dear to my heart).

Thinking about the challenges and possible gains of graduate work created my mixed feelings when I learned that I was admitted into the Ph.D. program. By then I had two small sons whose chances to gain a socially and academically empowered future now depended on me. Graduate school was a major step, as it represented an opportunity to fight for academic legitimacy of our cultural voice. But my terror materialized when I finally dared to formulate my cultural insight in a term paper assignment. I wrote about Chicano youth gangs, critiquing the clinical approach of contemporary analyses, and proposed that adherence to traditional culture operated to reduce conflict. My professor reprimanded me for my irreverence to my colonizer's rules, which included a ban on the re-examination of my own cultural community. In big, red letters he wrote on the front page of my paper that it was not representative of graduate-level work because it was naively emotional, not analytical. Thus I was warned to improve my schoolwork by denying my native viewpoint. Within academia he was an established, well-respected expert on culture and deviance. I was alone, naive, and lacked a support system within the school. His power loomed over me as I imagined and feared institutional retribution in the form of expulsion from the graduate program and tried to conform in my subsequent work by sounding like someone else. I struggled to understand the theories presented in my books and classes and to find merit in them. I succeeded only in learning to imitate them, by mimicking their language and tracing their logic. Ultimately my professor's reaction silenced my cultural voice through most of my graduate years, subordinating it through the power inherent in a pedagogy that supports academia's hegemonic epistemologies, denying legitimacy to the native version of truth.

My graduate education included rigorous training in European social anthropology and its legacy to the discipline in the United States. I read and struggled with the theories of Tylor, Radcliffe-Brown, Levi-Strauss, Barth, Firth, Forte, Malinowski, Durkheim, and others that in readings and seminars were treated as sacred texts. Their epistemological power was secularized and thus legitimated by an intellectual rhetoric that carefully guarded against the destabilizing potential of counter-discourses. Although poststructuralist, postmodernist theories had come into the academic scene, they were not integrated into nor even acknowledged by UCLA's graduate studies in anthropology. Other anthropologists, including Morgan, Boaz, Stewart, Benedict, and Mead were praised as mavericks of their time. Mead became my hero. She was as close to a renegade as my academic confinement allowed me to know. Once, I attended a talk she gave at UCLA and admired her outspoken viewpoints on issues that made her unpopular with academic conservatives. But even Mead's work supported the status quo because she was a privileged white academic whose status empowered her voice, and her work modified but did not transform anthropological theory and method. Having been so embedded in the web of academic colonization, it was only after years of frustration, isolation, and alienation that I learned about Foucaultian notions of power and the promise of liberation inherent in the production of postcolonial discourse.

The privileged socialization of nonminority students and exclusion of minority students from the sources of power are integral to the process of domination. As a minority graduate student, I was not privy to social membership or dialogue in the student groups within the department. As had happened when I was introduced to university culture, I could only observe and eavesdrop as an invisible outsider.

The department also formalized my invisibility by refusing me consideration for fellowships and assistantships, thus denying me the benefits of professional training that these offer. Although my grades, and the recommendation of faculty, qualified me for a teaching assistantship, I never received one though I applied almost every year. The departmental secretary fielded my questions, evading my queries about the channels of authority, the process of decision-making, or the faculty involved in selection committees. I was told only that selection was not on a "need" basis. Thus I was reminded of my status as an Other, that I was not an equal but merely a product of academic charity. Being excluded from awards not based on "need" also meant that I was considered to be not intellectually up to par. The awards were given repeatedly to the same students. Ironically, in at least one case, I finished my dissertation years ahead of my T.A!

I learned from being subjected to these forms of exclusion how the academy cedes to the pressure of public demands for reform by granting us formal admission but this does not include socially legitimated space. I secretly admired the militancy of politically active students I had noticed around school and the bonds of support that they seemed to share. My faculty mentor, himself a Chicano struggling to survive within the academy, was my single lifeline. I benefited from his empathy and his insistence on connecting with the other two Chicana graduate students in the department. He encouraged us to provide each other support, and demanded that we work hard, read everything, question critically, and never allow ourselves to believe we knew enough. Our unprecedented admission into the anthropology department contributed to a sharing of experiences and special bonding from which the longest lasting friendship in my life grew. The special value of this friendship, as well as the reason I remain so fond of my former mentor, is due to the fact that he and the other Chicana helped cultivate my intellectualism and provided me with cultural refuge from the estrangement I found within the academy.

In my quest for an improved future and my concerted efforts to survive the rigors of my education, I was not conscious of the distance from my family and community that this process was creating. I realized this the day I explained to my mother the reasons for my divorce. They were grounded in an academically informed logic that to my mother meant mere foreign words sounding suspiciously like pretexts that could not justify the break from tradition and from the commands of God. My family of origin attributed my divorce to the strain that my academic work had caused in my marriage by keeping me from my domestic and maternal duties. My achievements thus were debunked by the same people whose approval and pride in me I had sought to gain.

While conducting my dissertation field research I also awoke to the fact that formal education empowers us in the eyes of our own community and thus separates us from it. I had relocated to the midwest and resided in an area very distant from where Latinos are concentrated. After months of loneliness I found out about a local group of Tarascan migrant farmworkers and eagerly and naively decided to base my study on them. I assumed that they would accept me and that I could give back something to my own community through this study. But gaining their trust was not as easy as I had anticipated. In the process of interviewing a woman I deeply respected, she became quite irritated with me and told me with a flushed face and a loud, angry tone that my questions made me sound like an immigration official or something similar and that if I wanted the cooperation of the other people in her community, I needed to abandon this approach and these questions. I recoiled immediately, recognizing the righteousness of her words and realizing the selfishness of my purpose in those questions. My motives were based on promoting my career. I had learned well how to trace a logic I did not believe and by using it I had reproduced the process of cultural imperialism. I had presumed her acceptance of me without the right to do so. I had no personal knowledge of her undocumented immigrant farmworking life, and being Mexican did not qualify me also as Tarascan, nor intimately acquaint me with Tarascan reality. As a student of culture I had intruded upon and scrutinized their lives and violated their privacy by documenting it and exposing it to my committee at UCLA, strangers with mysterious lives, residing two thousand miles away, yet they would pass judgment on the lives of the people I presented. Had I followed my cultural instincts I would have resisted and refused to perform these actions, and in that way maintained what cultural closeness I did share with this woman and her community. This incident and the one with my family over my divorce sparked a profound sadness that enveloped me because I knew then that my education cost more than a good deal of time and money. It cost me my cultural identity and my sense of belonging. I was no longer the same daughter, wife, sister, mother, or friend I once had been. Nor was I accepted by academia. This left me feeling as if I did not belong anywhere at all. The words of my mentor speaking of how academic life affected those of us new to it rang true in my head. This was indeed a very lonely, alienating life.

I learned to imitate academic language and logic well enough to win research grants, get job interviews, and speak in professional conferences. Hence, my career began to take form in the typical way. But colonization left me deeply scarred with insecurity from which I was not soon to recover. When I was offered my first job I did not turn it down in spite of what my instincts told me. Academic employment was scarce and I was afraid I might never find another job. Yet I had secretly hoped not to receive the offer. I had no clue as to how to organize a class, what readings to use or why or how. The academic material remained for me too illogical, too foreign, and too incomprehensible. As Perez (1993, 54) has pointed out, learning to master the language of survival is not the same as owning the language of the conqueror. So I felt ignorant. In retrospect, these problems surfaced because of my inner conflict with academia in general and anthropology in particular. As a teacher I would be expected to convey information that I believed to be true, and I did not. I did not believe that education made us free, because mine had bound me; I did not believe that the native voice was unworthy, because I loved and respected my culture; and I did not believe that anthropology was truly culturally relativistic because I had witnessed its imperialist practice. I was only in love with a philosophy that had no tangential reality. And I was at a loss as to how to deal with this complexity within myself, and worse, how to reconcile this in my writing and teaching. I no longer had my mentor's advice, for he had accepted a position in another institution, and my new committee chair made it a practice to treat me with condescension and thus discouraged me from seeking her help or advice. I also lacked the teaching practice that other graduate students gained as teaching assistants. These conflicts and lack of experience compounded the problematic transition from student to professional. I was unpolished, had not developed technique nor style, and I had no idea what lay ahead.

My first teaching disaster occurred in my first term. My course lacked clear objectives, coherence, and I was not in control of the class. The classroom was a sea of stern white faces, which raised my fears, resentments, and insecurities borne in my student years. I tried to convey anthropological principles but did so with serious apprehension. A group of opportunistic students quickly detected my weaknesses and bore in on them, and I spent a semester dealing with racial harassment and abuse, feebly disguised at times as normal classroom playfulness, at others more blatantly displayed. Such treatment from the students was reflective of that which I received from my peers. I was ignored in the hallways, left sitting at my desk as the rest of the faculty paraded by my office to hold lunchtime departmental meetings, and denied any form of salutation when I returned from a semester of maternity leave, proudly displaying my baby girl. By then I had drawn the conclusion that white academics seemed rude because they lacked the cultural emphasis on politeness that my own culture taught me, and that academia, dominated by a white, middle-class culture, frowned upon and interpreted politeness as weakness. (In fact I have tested this theory at conferences, where I have found that people to whom I smilingly say pleasantries soon assume an arrogant tone with me). But the demoralization that the behavior of the other faculty was meant to produce in me eventually took hold. One faculty member finally admitted to me that I had been forced upon the department by the administration, who had required them to select the female minority in the applicant pool, and the department's efforts to sabotage that decision had failed. The nature of my appointment had engendered their anger and, along with my teaching deficiencies, provided them justification for not treating me as an equal. The institution thus had demonstrated its apparent commitment to affirmative action, but, once again, this would be qualified by lack of social acceptance that within the department and the institution would deny me equitable participation.

The job announcement for a position at another institution indicated a preference for an expert on Latinos. Although this was a combined sociology and anthropology department, and I would be the only full-time anthropologist in the department, and the prospect of good employment and the opportunity to nurture my interests in my own community excited me and filled me with optimism. But being a Latina(o) and being an expert on Latinos have different significance in academia. The two are viewed as mutually exclusive, as became evident as soon as I began my new position.

My first term did not go well. Student evaluations placed me well below the departmental mean, with comments conveying their disapproval, dislike, and disdain. Several comments claimed I was "unapproachable," and that I made too many references to Latin Americans. This sounded all too familiar, and I had not learned to cope with it any better. But I was determined to survive because I felt that I had too much invested. The student ratings and comments were noted in my first annual review and I was asked to address them. I assumed the responsibility and attributed the negative student ratings to my period of adjustment. The department approved my contract renewal for the next academic year, although noting that my teaching needed improvement.

The following quarter I had my best teaching experience ever. Students were friendly, receptive, and I was having a great time. This was the magic that had been missing, it seemed, because my evaluations rose above the mean of the department. I gained a taste of what being a teacher really could be like. Subsequent evaluations did not go as well, and a number of angry and biased comments still accompanied a rating of my classes lower than the mean, although they did not return to the level shown in my first term.

During that first year at I conducted a study in two of Chicago's Latino communities with quite a respectable grant from the Inter-University Program for Latino Research. I had learned to give importance to my native insight and reflected this into my study objectives and methods, carefully selecting and training my field research assistants (two throughout the project, seven in total, all bilingual and Latino). With some trepidation, I began to believe that in time I could carve a comfort zone within academia. Then I found out I was pregnant again, and I took part of the following year to delight in and nurture my newborn son.

When I returned in the spring quarter I faced a formal peer review that melted my hopes and fantasies with a familiar reality. In this review I was asked; 1) to account for the negative student evaluations in terms of their claim about my disorganization, as shown by my tendency to refer to more than one ethnographic reading or example in the same topic; 2) to explain my teaching methods, objectives, and materials; 3) whether I gave my own views and perspectives when students asked for them; and 4) why four or five of forty-five student evaluations had shown serious dissatisfaction with my teaching and grading.

This was a process in disempowerment. It represented an inquisition in which censorship prohibited pedagogical autonomy and creativity, as can be seen in a close examination of each review issue. First, referring to the use of more than one ethnographic example as pedagogical "disorganization" discredits what is, in fact, a skill needed in a cultural anthropology course—to introduce students to the idea of examining issues in various cultural contexts, to help them understand the importance of crosscultural comparison, and to gain an appreciation of cultural difference and specificity. Second, asking faculty to discuss teaching methods, objectives, and materials is useful when the purpose is to evaluate constructively, such as to generate and share ideas to improve our coursework. This was not the intent in my case, however. Implicitly, a review that requires such an accounting invalidates a priori the particular faculty member's choice of teaching objectives, methods, and materials. Third, asking a faculty member whether he or she responds truthfully when students ask for our views and perspectives implies that teaching is totally value-free when in fact, it is loaded with the biased baggage that our own academic training and life experience have given us. The question demonstrates suspicion and fear of how this baggage can inform a discourse that will upset the status quo. And four, emphasis on the negative, rather than the positive, shows a manipulation of the meaning of student evaluations.

The humiliating nature of faculty reviews is reinforced by the inclusion of students in what I believe should be a privately held process. The department invited two students to participate in my review, including the period during which I left the room for the department to deliberate. These students also conducted a "random" telephone survey among students in my classes which the two students used to rate my teaching performance and base their own vote in the department's decision regarding contract renewal. Neither the participation of the two students nor the survey was explained to me prior to the review meeting. The presence of these students throughout the faculty deliberation of my case was a flagrant violation of my privacy. Such practices put into question our professional integrity, blemishing our image in the eyes of those whose respect we dedicate our lives to earn. Proving the Foucaultian notion that where there is power there is resistance, my internal response to why the five students showed dissatisfaction was (*porque esos cabrónes, huevones no aprecian lo que se les ofrece y no merecen perder el tiempo de los demás, y ustedes son muy pendejos para reconocerlo!*) but I answered aloud: "Four or five out of forty-five? I think I'm doing pretty well!" Heresy. After a silent moment, apparently to digest my impiety, the department turned to questions about my university service and my research, in both cases discrediting them a priori as Latino-centered activities. I was asked to describe what I "do" besides attend meetings, in the Latino committees on which I serve in the university (specifically, these include the Latin American Studies faculty committee and the steering committee of the Center for Latino Research). The racism that permeates academia was clearly demonstrated in the department's indulgence of this question. As it did not merit a reasonable answer, I did not give one. My retort was "I do what we all do at committees . . . what do you do?"

Finally, a senior faculty member asked what my theoretical position was in my research. Such a question belongs in a job interview and not in a yearly review, especially when the validity of our work has been established through the academic scrutiny that precedes funding awards. Significantly, the Inter-University Program has a Latino power base, which tends to strike suspicion with mainstream departments. When, in response, I invoked the work of Del Castillo, Anzaldúa, Zavella, and more, the faculty member interrupted me (as I recall his words), "I don't know those names, so could you tell us where you are in a broader, more familiar sense?" While presenting my answer I mentioned Marxist-feminist theory, to which he sighed a signal that he understood my response.

The department majority voted against my contract renewal. Reasons included my "failure to improve teaching performance," an inability to spark sufficient student interest in anthropology, and lack of academically productive activities.

These explanations demonstrate the subjective and arbitrary nature of review processes, the outcomes of which depend on who judges whom and how academic endeavors of minority faculty are regarded by the mainstream. The point about my productivity, for example, denied the value of a year-long ethnographic study, the "productivity" of which is shown in the fact that it was funded with a grant equal to one half of my yearly salary, was conducted in my first year in this institution, involved seven Latino student research assistants and provided these students a learning experience and an opportunity to work within their own communities. In addition, the implicit expectation that I should have been "producing" academically while on maternity leave revealed a sexist, classist attitude that devalues the demands inherent in the motherhood role and the right to reproductive freedom, belying any departmental claim to a commitment to feminist and social equality principles. Furthermore, the use of student evaluations also evidences how minority faculty can be forced out by the manipulation of review criteria. For example, the student ratings that in my class superseded the departmental mean and comments praising my teaching were given no acknowledgment at all by the department. On the other hand, complaints that I "assign too much reading" or "refer to Latin Americans too much" formed the basis of decisions determining the future of my career.

The cover of guaranteed anonymity in student evaluations invites the expression of unqualified statements imbued with racist, classist, and sexist attitudes and perceptions. If such statements were openly made, their obvious biases would render them unusable as review material. Yet when a number of such statements are made under the protection of anonymity, they are validated as indications of the instructor's failure to provide students with a positive classroom experience. In looking over the individual, anonymously written justifications that faculty gave for deciding my case, at least one claimed that racism did not constitute an issue in student evaluations, especially among the "more seasoned students." Such a claim demonstrates how even departments composed of "seasoned" experts in the areas of society and culture fail to acknowledge the inappropriateness of standardized evaluations, demonstrating the department's own biases and how these control and ultimately determine the academic body and the degree of participation of minority faculty. The misuse of student evaluations also reflects the panic in academia over current political and bureaucratic demands for financial accountability. Such demands encourage departments to cater to student satisfaction in an effort to increase student enrollment and discourage the production of critical thought.

The politics of representation, the use of students as instruments of domination, the hegemonic power of mainstream epistemology, the subordination of the native voice, all are evident and articulated in the formalized practice of faculty reviews. The reviews demonstrate institutional and departmental lack of commitment to minority faculty retention by the use of the same criteria to judge the performance and contributions of minority and nonminority faculty. This is not equality. This is domination through the imposition of privileged philosophies and ideologies expressed in values and expectations that do not acknowledge the effects of oppression, disempowerment, and exclusion of minority experiences. Such practices do not allow affirmative action to rectify the status of minorities because of the biased criteria that are used to determine our "fit" within departments and institutions.

My own shortcomings have contributed to how I have experienced academia and I must acknowledge my own complicity in the processes to which I have alluded. When I accepted my employment at the second institution, I felt I was prepared to deal with the politics of academia and with its academic requirements. I was wrong. I still had not come to terms with the conflicts created by my education. When my first courses were reviewed they lacked direction, topical cohesion, and my teaching was devoid of my Self. Through most of my teaching career, until very recently, I have allowed the voice of my colonizer to subordinate my own, failing to confront biases and thus succumbing to the fear of retribution. Only hesitantly have I introduced students to my own cultural knowledge, hardly sharing with them the excitement of my research, or what I know of the Latino(a) experience. I did not dare to confront racism by calling it what it is. I have resisted too passively, only subconsciously, through the hesitation and apprehension with which I have delivered my lectures. I have maintained distance between my students and myself, following the examples of my own committee chair and other professors, who taught me to deal with the student-professor relationship in this way. Keeping this distance as a professor also helped mark my difference and affirmed my separation from students, whom I have viewed as representations of my colonizer. In these ways I have been involved in almost silent and unproductive resistance, attempting not too successfully to establish my independence and my own identity.

In the first act of open resistance since entering academia, I contested the proceedings of my review to my dean in a detailed letter that pointed out the racism and sexism with which I was treated. I was granted a contract renewal. But the formal review process left me demoralized and consciously aware that academic life is a struggle which I often feel like giving up. My children, and the legacy of cultural freedom and the right to be ourselves that I can leave them, still represent my inspiration in my decision to remain an academic. I have begun to work on a new struggle, one in which I am learning from people like hooks (1994), who teach us how to teach to transgress, and thereby redefine my relationship with students and facilitate the empowering of disempowered students. Recently, in my Introduction to Cultural Anthropology class, we were discussing how various peoples of the world utilize their ecological resources. Four Latino students, usually silent in class, lit up with broad smiles, and for the first time in class made direct eye contact with me and with each other, when I mentioned the savory aroma of frying tripitas. I had no question in my mind at that point that a professor's ability to "spark students' interest in anthropology" depends on whether we truly acknowledge the importance of different cultural realities, including the realities of the less represented students.

The terror is still part of my academic life, and I struggle constantly against it with a resistance that remains mainly subjectified. When I wonder whether my resistance needs to be outward to be significant, I get inspired again by the people who mean the most to me, such as my mother. She recently wrote me a letter, in which she enclosed some handwritten home remedies she has taken to copying out of alternative medicine books. I had looked upon this sadly as an indication that using those books was undermining my mother's intimate cultural knowledge of traditional Mexican medicinal plants. My fears were relieved when I read what she wrote (in this case, she had found a recipe for slenderness, to help me regain my figure after the birth of my baby): "After gathering enough nettle, wash it in cold water. Use kitchen tongs to remove from water. Allow to drain on paper towels for a few minutes before refrigerating . . . *yo no sé cual es esa planta . . . a lo mejor son nopales*"!

Note

Yes, I am Mexicana, Latina, Chicana, woman, daughter, mother, wife, friend, but also I am a teacher in a world very different from the one in which I was born and in which I was formed as a human being. So now it appears that I am neither what I was, nor what I appear to be.

Reference List

hooks, bell. 1994. Teaching to Transgress: Education as the Practice of Freedom. Routledge. New York.

Pérez, Emma. 1993 Sexuality and Discourse: Notes from a Chicana Surivior. In: Chicana Critical Issues. Mujeres Activas en Letras y Cambio Social. Series in Chicana/Latina Studies. Third Woman Press. Berkeley. pp. 45–69.

West, Cornel. 1993. The New Cultural Politics of Difference. In: The Cultural Studies Reader. Simon During, Ed. Routledge. London/New York. pp. 203–207.

Chapter 13

Doing Battle Inside the Beast

Luis Ortiz-Franco

Introduction

This story describes my experiences in my attempt to attain tenure at a private liberal arts four-year university in California. This anecdote vividly illustrates the need to retain and enforce antidiscrimination policies like affirmative action in academic institutions in order to guarantee fair opportunity to ethnic minorities. The events that unfolded in my experience also illustrate what many social scientists, past and present, have maintained: that social change is the result of the struggle between two opposing, and sometimes antagonistic, forces.

Although the events that are described here took place in a private university, similar incidents happen in public academic institutions as well, and the struggle to maintain affirmative action in those institutions is sometimes very dramatic. As I write this narrative in the autumn of 1995, a group of Latino undergraduate students at the University of California Irvine (UCI) are risking their lives through a water-only fast to protest the abolishment of affirmative action programs in admissions, hiring, and contracting within the University of California (UC) by the UC Board of Regents. The UC Regents repealed the affirmative action mandates because they claimed that the goals and objectives of those antidiscrimination policies had already been met. Moreover, the regents reasoned that the implementation of those mandates was perpetuating the social ills that they were designed to correct because white males were now being discriminated against due to their race and gender. In opposition, the protesting students demand the reinstitution, and expansion of affirmative action programs because, they argue, discrimination against minorities and women still persists within the UC system and in society at large.

This narrative supports the arguments of the protesting Latino UCI undergraduates, since the events described here demonstrate that qualified members of historically underrepresented groups in the United States constantly face zealous discrimination by members of the white majority. Despite the demagogic claims of many individuals, we still have miles and miles to go before we live in a color-blind society as dreamed of by Dr. Martin Luther King.

This narrative is organized as follows: The first section, Antecedents, provides some general background about the experience of the author from graduate school to the time leading up to the events described here. The second section, The Setting, is divided into several parts: general information about the academic institution where the events took place; the institution's requirements for granting tenure; a statement of my record; and the decision rendered by the faculty committee assigned to evaluate petitions for tenure. The third section, Reversing the Decision, describes the actions and events triggered by the initial decision on my petition for tenure and the eventual outcome of the process. The fourth and last section, Conclusions, outlines some of the lessons learned from my experience.

Antecedents

When I received my Ph.D. degree in Mathematics Education from Stanford University in 1977, I was relatively optimistic about my chances for getting a teaching job in a four-year college or university in the United States. Even though I was aware of some of the politics in obtaining academic appointments, including discrimination against minorities and women, I was very hopeful that the white professors who control the search and selection process in colleges and universities would value my accomplishments and give me an opportunity to launch an academic career.

At the time I received my Ph.D., the Stanford School of Education was rated the best in country. Furthermore, I was one of a handful of Latinos in the United States specializing in mathematics education, and I was the only Latino, and Chicano, to have received a doctorate in mathematics education from Stanford in the entire history of the institution. Moreover, the vast majority of academic institutions in the country had an affirmative action program, at least on paper, for academic hiring. Despite all these factors, I did not get a postsecondary teaching position during the first nine years after receiving my doctorate, even though I applied to no fewer than one hundred colleges, universities, and community colleges throughout the country.

The common reasons given in the letters rejecting my applications for teaching positions were that I was not qualified, or that they had selected someone else more qualified than me. Those reasons rang hollow and untrue because I rarely applied for jobs for which I was not qualified. Over time, I became convinced that the faculty search committees were not judging me by my academic accomplishments, but by my ethnic and cultural background. However, I never gave up my dream of someday becoming a college or university professor.

In the interim, however, I worked as a grant writer and research coordinator for academic institutions, as an educational researcher in a private think-tank and for the U.S. Department of Education. I also worked for the late César Chavez assisting America's farmworkers. In the process, I learned some valuable survival skills, one of which was to adopt a strong psychological and optimistic outlook in the face of discrimination and rejection, skills that proved to be valuable in my struggle for tenure.

The Setting

The Academic Institution

I teach in a four-year private liberal arts university established in California in 1861. Over the years, it changed both its name and location several times before settling in its current site in southern California in the 1950s, and adopting its current name in the early 1990s. The geographical area where the university is located has the reputation of being a "hostile zone" for ethnic minorities in particular.

When I started teaching at that university in 1986, there were no members of historically underrepresented American minorities (African-Americans, Latinos, and Native Americans) in either the faculty or administrative ranks, and there were no student organizations specifically representing the interests of the few African-American and Latino students on campus. In fact, when I interviewed for the job, I was asked if I would be interested in becoming the faculty advisor of a Latino student organization if such a group formed.

At that time, the entire student body consisted of about 1,600 students, and there were about 110 full-time faculty members in the tenure track professional classification. The students and faculty at the university have historically been insulated from interacting with minorities as their teachers or colleagues, as is the case in most institutions of higher learning.

When I accepted the offer to teach at the university, I shared my decision with a friend who teaches anthropology, and she commented that I was venturing into "the belly of the beast." Soon after I was hired as a nontenured associate professor on tenure track, I focused on doing the best job I could in a number of different areas: teaching; publishing (both refereed and nonrefereed) articles and books; developing friendships with other faculty members; interacting with students; and getting involved in campus committees and in professional organizations. I also made it a point to establish contact with local Latino community organizations. As time went by, I learned the hard way to survive in an academic institution which was not supportive of minority academicians, for I faced nonacceptance by some white students, and obstacles were put in my way by other professors. However, there were a few faculty members who accepted my friendship and, as time went by, an increasing number of students both liked my teaching and appreciated the support I gave them in their academic endeavors and their extracurricular interests.

It was common for me to either set up special appointments for students to come to my office for academic assistance on an individual basis, or to arrange for groups of students to come to my office to discuss their mathematics homework. Although initially I did those things solely to help the students learn and experience success in mathematics, eventually those practices enabled many students to succeed in mathematics, contrary to their previous experiences with the subject, and they began to spread the word that I was the "best" mathematics teacher at the university. So, as my popularity increased, my student teaching evaluations also improved.

Simultaneously, I functioned as the faculty advisor of the Latino student organization on campus which formed shortly after my arrival, and I supported the members as much as I could in their social, cultural, and fundraising activities. I also served as a resource person to all students, Latino and non-Latino, who solicited from me letters of recommendation, or asked me for information about applications for scholarships, graduate school, campus jobs, and so on.

On the professional side, I published articles in refereed journals, and books in collaboration with other colleagues, and I got involved in local, national, and international professional groups dedicated to mathematics education. I also cultivated good working relationships with non-academic staff at the university.

I engaged in all those activities because I saw them as an integral part of being a faculty member, and I saw those activities as being congruent with the university's expectations for achieving tenure.

Institutional Expectations for Tenure

In the tradition of most liberal arts universities, the school where I teach values teaching more than it values research or publications. But the university also expects its faculty to engage in scholarly activities (or creative activities in the case of faculty in the fine arts department), as well as in community service in addition to teaching, all as part of their accomplishments for tenure consideration. In order of importance for tenure university-wide, teaching is the most important, followed by scholarly/creative activity, and then service.

In fact, official documents of the university indicate that the greatest weight among the three evaluative categories of teaching, scholarly/creative activity, and service is placed on teaching. Demonstrated teaching excellence is measured by student evaluations, where ratings range from 1 (lowest) to 5 (highest); excellence in teaching is necessary for achieving tenure.

With respect to scholarly/creative activity, as is the case in all colleges and universities, the number of publications required for tenure is not specified. What is also not specified at the university where I teach is the number of publications in refereed journals expected for the granting of tenure. This lack of specificity gives latitude to the institution when making decisions for tenure or promotion, and may at times favor the institution, and at other times the candidate for tenure, depending on the prevailing political winds. The official documented rhetoric indicates that, prior to tenure consideration, it is important that the faculty member establish a record of scholarly/creative accomplishments and show clear promise to continue to do so.

Regarding service, the institutional lingo simply states that a record of service to the university is also expected. In practice, that record includes service on campus committees, active participation in professional organizations, including participation in committees and presentations at conferences, contributions to improving the general life of the campus, and service to local community organizations outside the university. While not all faculty participate in all the various community levels, membership in professional committees at the national and international levels is most highly valued.

My Record for Tenure Consideration

I applied for tenure consideration at the beginning of the 1991–92 academic year, my sixth year at the university, with the following record: My overall average index of teaching excellence was 4.1 in the 1–5 scale, 1 being lowest and 5 highest.

Regarding scholarly/creative activity, I had sixteen publications: two books in conjunction with other authors, two articles in refereed journals, one short note in a refereed journal, two chapters in books, two articles based on empirical research in the national newsletters of academic organizations, one article published in an international newsletter in mathematics education, and the remaining articles placed in the ERIC files. I also had a record of fifteen presentations in professional conferences and had organized four conferences on mathematics education over the years.

With respect to service, my service to the university included participation as member and chair of faculty standing committees on campus, faculty advisor of the Latino student organization, active membership in national and international organizations in mathematics education, president and member of advisory boards in the Latino community off-campus, and consultant for profit and nonprofit organizations.

I distributed copies of my resume and my teaching record among those colleagues from whom I was seeking direct and indirect support.

The Decision on Tenure

When I submitted my request for tenure consideration, in addition to my record described in the previous section, I included in my file letters of support from senior faculty members from several departments with whom I had either worked harmoniously in faculty committees or with whom I had developed a friendly and collegial relationship over the years. Moreover, both the chair of my department and the chair of the natural sciences division, the academic division which houses the Mathematics Department, wrote letters in support of my petition for tenure.

The faculty committee charged with reviewing and evaluating the requests for tenure and promotion was made up of seven tenured faculty members: two of them were from the same academic division as I was; two faculty were from the social sciences division; one was from music; another was from the humanities; and another professor was from physical education. Although the proceedings and deliberations in the meetings of that committee are supposed to be confidential, bits and pieces filtered to various faculty members around campus subsequent to the committee's decision. I found out that the committee had taken an unusually long time to arrive at a decision on my case. The apparent reason for that delay was that a member of the committee was doing everything possible to convince other committee members to deny my request for tenure. Most committee members, at one point, were resisting the influence of that colleague because they were finding it difficult to justify a negative decision in the face of the evidence before them. Eventually, the forces of unfairness overcame the tendency for fairness and the committee voted four to three against granting me tenure.

When I received the letter from the committee on February 3, 1992, informing me of their decision, I was stunned, to say the least. As soon as I received the letter communicating to me the adverse decision, I shared the bad news with all those faculty members who had written letters supporting my request for tenure, and with other faculty members who over the years had always supported me. All of them were as taken aback by the decision as I was, and a few of them even broke down privately in my presence.

Concurrently, I shared the bad news with the Latino students whom I had spent many hours mentoring, advising, and otherwise supporting in their extracurricular activities. Some of those students pointedly asked me if I thought I was being discriminated against. My answer to that question was unequivocal: yes, I thought I was being discriminated against, because I was qualified to receive tenure.

The struggle to reverse the adverse decision took sixteen months. In the process, many people who had never before participated in social action became social activists on campus.

Reversing the Decision

Phase I: Staying Alive

The news that I had been denied tenure spread rapidly across the campus, and within a couple of days students, faculty, and staff began showing their support for me in various ways. They knew that I was being discriminated against and wanted to show their disagreement with the action taken. In the first four months following the committee's adverse decision, the following events took place:

Meetings occurred between nonacademic staff and the president of the university in which the nonacademic staff expressed their support for me and asked the president to act in a socially responsible way to reverse the discriminatory decision against me. When some of those staff people told me of their actions, I thanked them for their support and told them that I admired their courage for potentially risking their jobs.

On another front, groups of students, Latinos, African Americans, Whites and Asians, on their own initiative, began to organize support groups. Soon thereafter, student group after student group met with the president of the university to urge him to reverse the adverse decision against me and to grant me tenure. They provided him detailed information, through personal anecdotes, about my teaching effectiveness. They shared with the president their knowledge of my commitment and dedication to their academic progress and my determination to teach mathematics to all those who wanted to learn.

The students told the president of the university about all those countless hours in my office when I guided group learning sessions during and after my official office hours. Many of them testified to the president of gaining self-confidence in their ability to learn mathematics, thus increasing their confidence to perform other academic work, thanks to their positive learning experience in my courses. Yet, the president would not accede to their request.

Simultaneously, some faculty members immediately formed a support committee that began soliciting support from other faculty to explore ways to reverse the adverse decision. They circulated a petition among the faculty and, after obtaining signatures of faculty from a cross section of the departments throughout the university, they presented the petition to the president. The faculty support committee also went to their respective departments and solicited participation from their colleagues to reverse the unfair discriminatory action concerning my tenure. Still, the institution would not reverse the decision considered by the majority of the local campus community to be unfair and discriminatory.

Then, suddenly, all went quiet on campus with respect to my case. Because I had not had anything to do with the activities of the previous months, I did not know what was going on. I wondered if people had given up on their efforts to turn a negative decision into a positive one without accomplishing their objective. At that point, my survival instincts took over. I decided that it was time to put into practice some of the lessons on social organizing that I had learned from farm labor leader César Chavez.

After some reflection, I concluded that to rekindle interest in my case, I needed concrete information to show my supporters, and I needed to issue a call for some type of action. To that end, I distributed copies of my resume to those students I knew had actively supported my case in the activities already described here. I told them that the copy of my resume was intended to provide them with information on my qualifications. The students welcomed this new information.

I also made a one-page anonymous flyer succinctly outlining my qualifications relevant to the tenure issue. That flyer also urged campus members to support a faculty member who cared about their education and their institution. I placed those flyers in strategic spots around campus where I knew students would pick them up. Also, I put copies of the flyer in the campus mail boxes of many faculty members.

Simultaneously, some members of the off-campus Latino community were holding sessions with student groups on campus in which issues of racism and discrimination were being discussed. Although I was not aware of these sessions at the time, I later learned that many students, Latinos and non-Latinos, were attending those sessions. All those uncoordinated activities precipitated more actions on my behalf on campus before the end of the school year.

Towards the end of the spring semester, students began writing articles in the school newspaper about my case and about affirmative action. Moreover, at a public meeting on campus, for which the board of trustees was hosting many community dignitaries, the students held a rally and a march in support of my case in plain view of the meeting participants. That action catapulted my case beyond the walls of the university. There was a brief mention of it in the local newspapers and on the local television station.

On the faculty side, leaders of the faculty approached me and recommended to me that I file a grievance against the faculty committee that had denied my petition for tenure. They told me that was the only way to keep my case alive. Moreover, they assured me that another faculty committee would review my grievance to determine if my case indeed merited an investigation. They also warned me that some faculty would give me the cold shoulder if I filed a grievance because they would interpret my action as questioning their judgment. I followed their recommendation about filing a grievance, and I kept their warnings in mind.

At the beginning of that summer (1992), I filed a grievance requesting reconsideration of my petition for tenure. In my grievance, I argued that the faculty committee that had denied me tenure had based its decision on inadequate consideration of my record, and they had violated affirmative action guidelines. The filing of the grievance permitted me to remain academically alive, at least until the grievance was resolved.

When I filed the grievance, I prepared myself to be isolated by some of the faculty. In preparation of that eventuality, I made the decision that instead of overreacting I would not antagonize anyone, and I would be polite and courteous with all my colleagues whenever I interacted with them. I was determined to win allies instead of making enemies. Moreover, I convinced myself that I was acting correctly and that I would fight for my case to the end, whatever that might be. I was determined not to compromise on the issue of tenure, because I deserved to achieve it.

Moreover, I channeled my stress and anxiety into writing articles on mathematics education in the Latino culture. In retrospect, as I was writing about mathematics in the Latino culture, I was burrowing myself into my culture and drawing strength from it to survive the struggle. And survive I did.

Phase II: The Final Stretch

By the end of the summer of 1992, the faculty committee that had been assigned to assess the merits of my grievance ruled in my favor and recommended that a grievance committee be formed to undertake a full investigation of my case. A faculty grievance committee composed of five members was formed to investigate my grievance. That committee conducted its investigations throughout the fall semester (1992), and rendered its decision in early 1993. While that committee was conducting its investigations, students were actively finding ways of expressing their support for me.

One group of students drafted a petition to the president of the university demanding that I be given tenure because, in their view, I was a good teacher and I deserved tenure. Another group of students made its presence known to the faculty grievance committee by showing up outside the rooms in which the committee met and carrying signs calling for affirmative action.

In addition, other groups of students continued to meet with the president of the university to urge him to grant me tenure. Some other students had their parents call the president of the university urging him to rule in my favor, and other students had their parents talk to members of the board of trustees about my case. Moreover, some local Latino community leaders who had heard about my case contacted the president of the university to register their support for me.

By then it was clear to everybody involved in the case, the board of trustees, the president of the university, students, faculty, university staff, my family, and the surrounding community, that the university was not an island, and that the institution had to answer in some way to all those campus and off-campus constituencies. Contemporaneous with many of the events mentioned above, I was informed that one of the members of the committee that had initially denied my request for tenure was lobbying very zealously for the faculty grievance committee to rule against me. I later learned that two members of the grievance committee, faculty members who were supposedly liberal and open-minded, did not consider racist some negative student comments which alluded to negative racial stereotypes about me and my teaching. However, the momentum was in my favor, and the grievance committee, on a 3–2 vote, ruled in early 1993 that my request for tenure should be reconsidered.

My case was immediately referred to the committee in charge of reviewing promotions and applications for tenure for academic year 1992–93. That committee was composed of seven members, three of whom were carryovers from the committee that had denied me tenure the year before. Again, the faculty member who had lobbied the grievance committee to rule against me also lobbied this new committee. However, this committee, in early spring 1993, voted 6–1 in my favor and expeditiously forwarded their recommendation to the president of the university to grant me tenure.

The president of the university delayed for two months forwarding his recommendation on my case to the board of trustees for ratification. However, finally, at the May 1993 meeting of the board of trustees, their last meeting of the academic year, the board of trustees approved the president's recommendation that I be awarded tenure. Thus, I became the first member of an historically underrepresented group to attain tenure in the 132-year history of this institution.

Conclusions

There are several conclusions that can be derived from the events described in this essay.

One conclusion is that a positive change in the struggle to bring diversity and fairness to academia in fact occurred at my university: a member of an historically underrepresented group attained tenure for the first time in the history of a one-hundred-plus-year-old university. This change occurred as a result of the struggle between two opposing and, at times, antagonistic forces: those supporting my application for tenure and those opposing me.

Another conclusion is that those members of historically underrepresented groups who contemplate achieving successful academic careers can learn some important lessons from my experience. In addition to building a strong academic record deserving of tenure, certain other foundational elements are also necessary in order to overcome discrimination in the tenure process.

First, it is necessary to establish a broad base of support within the campus community and the greater off-campus community. Second, it is necessary to cultivate the fact that most people, regardless of ethnicity, dislike unfairness and discrimination and are willing to support, in their own way, someone who is experiencing discrimination. Third, in order to win support whenever one finds himself or herself in a political struggle in academia, it is necessary to avoid antagonizing one's potential supporters and to increase the number of allies— that is, isolate the perpetrators of the discrimination. Fourth, one must reach within the culture and history of his or her people for inner strength to wage the struggle to its final conclusion. Finally, one must be convinced that he or she is fighting the good fight and is on the correct side in the struggle.

Despite the fact that white faculty members at my university profess to be committed to ethnic and cultural diversity in the faculty ranks, there are currently on tenure track only two other faculty who are members of historically underrepresented groups. One is an African American, and one is a Latino. I have shared with them my experiences, and the conclusions that I have reached in my tenure struggle at this university, both of which I anticipate will be useful in their academic careers.

Notes on Contributors

Marisa Alicea is an Associate Professor at DePaul University's School for New Learning. She teaches courses on valuing human differences and immigration. She has published articles concerning Puerto Rican and Latino immigration, and diversity issues. Her most recent publication is based on life history narratives of female heroin users.

Alicia Chavira-Prado received her Ph.D. in Anthropology from UCLA in 1987. Her specializations include: Cultural Anthropology, Applied Anthropology, and Latinos in the United States. Her research has been on the significance of gender in the creation of ethnic community, focusing on the roles of immigrant women in the survival of immigrant households.

Fassil Demissie is an Associate Professor, Urban Studies program, DePaul University. His main research interest is in the discourse of architecture and identity and his work has been published in *American Anthropologist, International Journal of Urban and Regional Research, Urban Studies*, and other journals. He is currently editing a book on the relationship between power and architecture.

Stephen Nathan Haymes an Assistant Professor, teaches social and cultural studies and philosophy of education at DePaul University, and is the author of *Race, Culture, and the City: A Pedagogy of Black Urban Struggle*, State University of New York Press.

Sandra Jackson is an Associate Professor in the School of Education, DePaul University. Her teaching and research interests include secondary education, curriculum, teaching writing and literature;

multiculturalism and gender in teaching and learning, and education in southern Africa. She is co-editor of the book *Beyond Comfort Zones in Multiculturalism: Challenging the Politics of Privilege as Educators*, published by Bergin and Garvey.

Gladys M. Jimé nez-Muñoz is an Assistant Professor of Women's Studies at the State University of New York at Oneonta. Her recent publications include: "The Elusive Signs of African-Ness: Race and Representation Among Latinas in the United States," in *Borderlines*; "Slips That Show and Tell: Fashioning Multiculture as a Problem of Representation in Education," co-authored book chapter in *Race, Identity and Representation in Education*, edited by Cameron McCarthy and Warren Crichlow, Routledge Press.

José Solís Jordán is an Assistant Professor at the University of Puerto Rico. He teaches educational foundations and liberal arts studies including feminism and women of color. His publications include: (co-edited) *Foundations of Educational Policy in the United States* (1989), Ginn Publishers, Needham Heights, Mass.; and authored *Public School Reform in Puerto Rico: Sustaining Colonial Models of Development* (1993) Greenwood Publishing Group, Westport, Conn.: co-edited *Beyond Comfort Zones* (1995) also with Greenwood. He is currently working on a history of Puerto Ricans in the Puerto Rican public schools under U.S. colonialism.

Xing (Lucy) Lu was born in China. Her Ph.D. is in Rhetoric and Communication which she received from the University of Oregon. An Assistant Professor, she is currently teaching International Communication, Small Group Communication, Rhetorical Criticism, and Persuasion in the Department of Communication of DePaul University. Author of *Rhetoric and Ancient China in the Fifth to Third Century B.C.E: A Comparison with Classical Greek Rhetoric* (forthcoming).

Aminah B. McCloud is an Associate Professor of Religious Studies at DePaul University. Author of *African American Islam*.

Claire Oberon Garcia is an Assistant Professor of English at the Colorado College, where she teaches Nineteenth Century American literature.

Luis Ortiz-Franco is an Associate Professor of Mathematics at the University of California, Los Angeles. He has worked as a research coordinator at the Chicano Research Center and has served as a volunteer staff member of the United Farm Workers under the late César Chávez.

K.E. Supriya is an Assistant Professor in the Department of Communication at The University of Wisconsin-Milwaukee. Her disciplinary focus is the intersection of Communications and Cultural Studies. Her theoretical interests include postcolonial feminism as it particularly informs questions of power, resistance, and identity as they manifest indiscursive, corporal, and material practices. Her teaching interests include multicultural and gender communications and the politics and practice of qualitative research methods.

Maria R. Vidal is an Associate Professor at Loyola University of Chicago. She teaches courses in the area of social welfare policy, community organizing, and race, ethnicity, and culture. She has published research concerning the economic incorporation of immigrants in the U.S., child welfare with Latino families, Latino political participation, welfare reform, and Latino family structure and process.

Studies in the Postmodern Theory of Education

General Editors
Joe L. Kincheloe & Shirley R. Steinberg

Counterpoints publishes the most compelling and imaginative books being written in education today. Grounded on the theoretical advances in criticalism, feminism and postmodernism in the last two decades of the twentieth century, Counterpoints engages the meaning of these innovations in various forms of educational expression. Committed to the proposition that theoretical literature should be accessible to a variety of audiences, the series insists that its authors avoid esoteric and jargonistic languages that transform educational scholarship into an elite discourse for the initiated. Scholarly work matters only to the degree it affects consciousness and practice at multiple sites. Counterpoints' editorial policy is based on these principles and the ability of scholars to break new ground, to open new conversations, to go where educators have never gone before.

For additional information about this series or for the submission of manuscripts, please contact:

Joe L. Kincheloe & Shirley R. Steinberg
637 West Foster Avenue
State College, PA 16801